X SAVES THE WORLD

X SAVES THE WORLD

HOW GENERATION X GOT THE SHAFT

BUT CAN STILL KEEP EVERYTHING FROM SUCKING

Jeff Gordinier

VIKING

VIKING
Published by the Penguin Group
Penguin Group (USA) Inc., 375 Hudson Street, New York, New York 10014, U.S.A. •
Penguin Group (Canada), 90 Eglinton Avenue East, Suite 700, Toronto, Ontario, Canada M4P 2Y3 (a division of Pearson Penguin Canada Inc.) • Penguin Books Ltd, 80 Strand, London WC2R ORL, England • Penguin Ireland, 25 St Stephen's Green, Dublin 2, Ireland (a division of Penguin Books Ltd) • Penguin Books Australia Ltd, 250 Camberwell Road, Camberwell, Victoria 3124, Australia (a division of Pearson Australia Group Pty Ltd) • Penguin Books India Pvt Ltd, 11 Community Centre, Panchsheel Park, New Delhi – 110 017, India • Penguin Group (NZ), 67 Apollo Drive, Rosedale, North Shore 0632, New Zealand (a division of Pearson New Zealand Ltd) • Penguin Books (South Africa) (Pty) Ltd, 24 Sturdee Avenue, Rosebank, Johannesburg 2196, South Africa

Penguin Books Ltd, Registered Offices:
80 Strand, London WC2R ORL, England

First published in 2008 by Viking Penguin,
a member of Penguin Group (USA) Inc.

10   9   8   7   6   5   4   3   2   1

Copyright © Jeff Gordinier, 2008
All rights reserved

A portion of this book first appeared on the Web site of the Poetry Foundation.

Portions of this book are based on the following articles published in *Details* magazine: "Has Generation X Already Peaked?" and "Yuppie 2.0," both copyright © 2006 Condé Nast Publications. Reprinted by permission. All rights reserved.

Library of Congress Cataloging-in-Publication Data

Gordinier, Jeff.
X saves the world : how Generation X got the shaft but can still keep everything from sucking / Jeff Gordinier.
   p.   cm.
ISBN 978-0-670-01858-1
1. Generation X—United States.   2. Conflict of generations—United States.
3. Popular culture—United States.   I Title.

HQ799.7.G67 2008
305.20973—dc22   2007025374

Printed in the United States of America
Set in Dante MT with Cg Gothic No 4
Designed by Daniel Lagin

For Julie, who's been waiting patiently

+

For Margot and Toby, who've been screaming their heads off

CONTENTS

A Disclaimer

The careful reader of *X Saves the World* might be prone to point out that the book contains its fair share of generalizations. (Pretty big ones, in some cases. Maybe even whopping.) The author is aware of this, and while he assures the reader that plenty of tireless legwork and traditional research have gone into the production of the work at hand, he concedes, too, that he has, yes, here and there, taken what we might call attitudinal liberties. Are *all* boomers venal sellouts? Are *all* millennials spotlight-craving airheads? (For that matter, are *all* Gen Xers nobly ironic individualists?) Well, of course not, even though the reader will notice that these generalizations do ring true on many surprising levels.

And that said, the author does not happen to agree with the gentleman from the *Washington Post*—a boomer, of course—who, in the spring of 2006, suggested that such generational generalizations are "baloney." The author prefers to think that the generalizations in *X Saves the World* are more along the lines of mortadella, which is that really expensive and delicious baloney they make in Italy.

—JSG

My life had become a series of scary incidents that simply weren't stringing together to make for an interesting book, and *God, you get old so quickly!* Time was (and is) running out.

—*Dag, in the chapter "Dead at 30 Buried at 70," from Douglas Coupland's 1991 novel* Generation X

Q: Do you like *American Idol?*
A: Come on! Who does not like *American Idol?* It's the best.

—*Excerpt from an interview with Frances Bean Cobain, age thirteen, in* i-D *magazine, January 2006*

How young are you?
How old am I?
Let's count the rings around my eyes.

—*The Replacements, "I Will Dare"*

INTRODUCTION:
CHECK YOUR HEAD

Do they make a pill for athazagoraphobia?

Athazagoraphobia.

You know the sensation, even if you don't know the word. You can look it up on one of those awesome Web sites devoted to phobias, where you'll find it listed along with fear of vegetables, fear of razors, and fear of the great mole rat. You'll probably see it right between fear of ruins and fear of atomic explosions, which is kind of perfect.

Athazagoraphobia tends to signify "an abnormal and persistent fear of being forgotten or ignored," so, if we're speaking generationally, we might think of it as akin to the anxiety that Molly Ringwald felt in *Sixteen Candles*. The fear of being passed over. Left behind. Blown off.

And, since we're speaking generationally, there's a good chance that you've been feeling that way over the past few years.

Might the term "Generation X" ring a bell? Well, in the event that you've forgotten, Generation X had a very good run between 1991 and 1999, but media curiosity about our reticent, dark-horse demographic began to dribble away at the end of the nineties. Right around the time of the dot-com meltdown, a stubborn old standby began to reassert itself. Once again it was time for a familiar spiel. Just the other day I got a press release for a PBS series called *The Boomer Century*. Here's what it said:

PBS Looks Back at a Generation That Transformed
America—And Leaps Forward to Predict Their Future—
In *The Boomer Century: 1946–2046*
*Rob Reiner, Oliver Stone, Erica Jong, Tony Snow, Dr. Andrew
Weil . . .*

SAN FRANCISCO, CA—The Who famously sang "I hope
I die before I get old" to their fellow Baby Boomers in "My
Generation," but with one of this demographic group's 78
million members turning 60 every eight seconds, they will
soon be the largest elder population in American history.
Will the nation's most closely observed generation simply
kick back in its later years, or keep breaking the rules?

Generation X has marinated in the fat of boomer mythology
for so long now that we're like Keanu Reeves in *The Matrix* when
he's hooked up to all those tubes and wires in a tub of gelatin. We
don't even notice. And yet the *relentlessness* of the juggernaut—
really, it's amazing. Pick up *Newsweek* and you'll come across a series called "The Boomer Files," which presses that creaky rewind
button one more time to tell us—*to teach us*—about all the astonishing changes the disco-and-Brie generation has wrought upon
the American lifestyle. Fashion, music, money, food, shopping,
parenting, sex—there is no realm of human conduct, *Newsweek*
avers, that remains unboomerized. A few sentences from the series
have stuck with me. The first, written by Peg Tyre, appears in a
story about a shocking discovery: it seems that when boomers fall
sick or get lonely, they often turn to their friends for help and support. *So smart!* I'm thrilled to hear that boomers have opened up
this new growth sector in interpersonal relationships, because until now, whenever I've been sick or lonely, I've usually dealt with
it by curling up in the garage with a bag of dog biscuits. But Peg's
nice enough to throw the rest of us a bone. "Boomers, of course,"
she writes, "didn't invent close friendships."

In a different installment of "The Boomer Files," David Gates, a fine critic and novelist, nevertheless delivers one of the baldest confessions of smug boomer solipsism you're likely to find. "Six months ago," he writes, "a friend played U2 for me for the first time. It was okay."

It was . . . *okay*.

There's a scene in *Half Nelson* that, for me, captures the boomers' incredible shrinking values. *Half Nelson* is a movie about a young white teacher named Dan Dunne, played naturally and brilliantly by Ryan Gosling, who can be found right in the trenches when it comes to "making a difference." During his work hours he teaches history and coaches basketball at an inner-city high school. In his spare time he smokes crack. Unlike the honky-savior pedagogues who usually populate these chalkboard movies, Dunne is a wreck: dumpy and disheveled, in debt, emotionally stunted, a junkie too clever for rehab.

But he still comes off better than his boomer parents do. At one point in the film Dunne goes home to see his mother, and the domestic tranquility of the scene is jarring: here you find a snapshot of Summer of Love pieties at their most cozy and cobwebbed. There is red wine, there is old music, there are we're-all-friends-here wisecracks about Ebonics, there is the inevitable "I'm still sexy like Susan Sarandon" earth-mama shimmy in the den. Gosling's character, who seems to be simmering at a low boil of disgust, goes to the kitchen, where his mother says, "Your father and I thought we were going to change the world when we were young, you know. What did *we* know?"

When it comes to changing the world, the boomers choked, but if we're to judge from the deluge of magazine covers and TV commercials these days, there is no hope of ignoring or diverting their grand march of triumph. Boomers are having sex! Staying young! Retiring in high style! Gearing up for their second act! Hey, fifty is the new thirty! *Right on, maaan!* You see this stuff everywhere, and you just know what's coming. David Crosby's face transplant.

The James Taylor/Carly Simon remake of *On Golden Pond*. Woodstock IV: Return to the Garden, cosponsored by Nike, Viagra, and Ben & Jerry's. The Brown Acid line of tie-dyed Depends. It's only a matter of time. The boomers are tucking in for another gluttonous, cheek-smeared, decade-long smorgasbord of self-importance. They're Botoxing their face-lifts. They're tidying up the cryogenic chambers. They're lining up a shaman and filling their iPods with Judy Collins and Procol Harum in preparation for their weeklong Hopi funerals in Sedona. Don't even try to escape.

X

All of which would be bad enough, except that now we've got an extra course to digest. When it's not obsessing over the mating habits of AARP members, the media beast has taken a fancy to another rising demographic cluster, the millennials, Gen Y, whose bloggy, bling-blingy birdsong of me-me-me sounds, to your beaten eardrums, a little bit like this:

> *Oh my God LindsayBritneyJessicaParis OMG OMG OMG OMG my boss Mr. Boring totally sucks because he told me he wouldn't promote me after THREE MONTHS but screw him because OMG Nick + Jessica R breaking up OMG I totally need that new Fendi purse OMG did you see that episode of LagunaBeachProjectRunwayAmericanIdol SO SO AMAZING anyway I don't care about Mr. Boring I'm gonna be CEO of Google by the time I'm 25.*

That's right. The boomers *bred*, and their solipsistic progeny have arrived just in time to serve Generation X a second helping of anxiety. To quote a brutally apt line from an LCD Soundsystem song, "I'm losing my edge. The kids are coming up from behind."

The millennials, spawned during the last days of disco, seem to speak with none of the doubt and skepticism that have marked—

and hampered—Generation X. They just *love* stuff. They love celebrities. They love technology. They love name brands. They're happy to do whatever advertising tells them to do. So what if they can't manage to read anything longer than a photo caption or an instant message—that's okay! If anything, it's an advantage. Because literacy leads to self-reflection and critical thinking, and self-reflection and critical thinking open the door to doubt and skepticism, and stuff like that just gets in the way when you're trying to get ahead, and *OMG did you see how fat Britney looks these days?!?!?!*

Let's take a look at February 12, 2007. That happened to be the publication date for two magazine cover stories that, in tandem, served to magnify the murmur of anxiety about the "echo boomers" (as they're occasionally called) and their pantyless weltanschauung. In *New York*, for a piece devoted to "Understanding the Greatest Generation Gap Since Rock and Roll," editors went with a photograph of a naked model photographing herself in bed and garlanded it with a flotilla of free verse: "i am not interested in privacy. online, I reveal everything—my breakups, my bank balance, my breakfast cereal, my body. my parents call it shameless. i call it freedom." Back over at *Newsweek*, Paris Hilton and Britney Spears flashbulbed their way into an exploration of "The Girls Gone Wild Effect: Out-of-Control Celebs and Online Sleaze Fuel a New Debate Over Kids and Values." "Something's in the air, and I wouldn't call it love," wrote Kathleen Deveny. "Like never before, our kids are being bombarded by images of oversexed, underdressed celebrities who can't seem to step out of a car without displaying their well-waxed private parts to photographers. . . . A recent *Newsweek* poll found that 77 percent of Americans believe that Britney, Paris, and Lindsay have too much influence on young girls. Hardly a day passes when one of them isn't making news. . . . Are we raising a generation of what one L.A. mom likes to call 'prosti-tots'?"

Which brings us back to athazagoraphobia. Because while the boomers and millennials have been siphoning up all this mass-media oxygen, somebody seems to have forgotten to put together the cover stories about Generation X turning forty. More to the point, somebody seems to have forgotten Generation X. We hear plenty about people in their teens and twenties, and even more about people in their fifties, but the stodgy old species known as the thirtysomething has been shuttled off, like Molly Ringwald herself, to some sort of Camp Limbo for demographic lepers. Could it be that the age group that popularized the phrase "jumped the shark" has done just that? Is Generation X already obsolete?

X

At this point maybe you're thinking, *Generation X—I always hated that term*. Just seeing it in print again is enough to make you feel as though you're passing a gallstone. I continue to stand in awe of Douglas Coupland's 1991 novel *Generation X: Tales for an Accelerated Culture*, the book that sent the moniker swarming across the media landscape like a mutant bug, and I am willing to bet that Coupland himself wouldn't mind seeing it scraped off his own windshield for the next forty years or so. Xers have always had a fondness for the circular argument ("The Pixies are so cool." "Actually the Pixies are not cool because they did that greedy reunion tour." "But they did the reunion tour in a very cool, self-conscious way." "But now it's become so obvious to love the Pixies that it's not cool to talk about them. Anyway, I was always more of a Gang of Four chick, myself . . ."), but in the case of the name Generation X, can we just leave it be? It's not something I want to waste space arguing about, because (1) it's too late to try to orchestrate a brand relaunch, and (2) as shorthand goes, we could do a lot worse.

Coupland originally came up with the term after reading Paul Fussell's 1983 book *Class: A Guide Through the American Status System*, which is a Cary Grantish meringue of social anthropology, and which ends with a chapter called "The X Way Out." There, Fussell suggests that America has a history of nurturing a class beyond class—a group of people whose tastes and habits wiggle free of the old hierarchies of money and social rank. "The young flocking to the cities to devote themselves to 'art,' 'writing,' 'creative work'—anything, virtually, that liberates them from the presence of a boss or supervisor—are aspirant X people, and if they succeed in capitalizing on their talents, they may end as fully fledged X types," Fussell writes. "X people constitute something like a classless class. They occupy the one social place in the U.S.A. where the ethic of buying and selling is not all-powerful. Impelled by insolence, intelligence, irony, and spirit, X people have escaped out the back doors of those theaters of class which enclose others."

You can see why Coupland was drawn to that.

Since Xers grew up in the leviathan shadow of the boomers, a sense of apartness played a role in forming our identity from the start. "Our little group has always been and always will until the end," as Kurt Cobain put it. And yet because of that apartness; because we're said to be the defiant demographic, dedicated to shredding whatever raiment the marketing apparatus tries to drape us in; because we'd prefer not to be categorized at all, thank you very much; because, like one of those unmarked speakeasies on the Lower East Side of Manhattan, we're not even supposed to acknowledge that we *exist*—coming right out and calling yourself an Xer has always seemed a bit too, I don't know, *Andrew McCarthy*. Too obvious.

I happen to have a folder full of Gen-X press clips from the early 1990s. If you ever need something that will goad you into getting around to scrubbing the toilet or surveying your tax returns, I would be more than happy to lend it to you. Open it, and within five minutes you'll be willing to do anything to get away. Your brain will atrophy. You will need to prop open your eyelids with habanero-flavored toothpicks. To pick up a magazine story about the subject in those years was to know, before even skimming it, that you were about to dunk your Doc Martens into a stagnant pond of clichés. Take the words below, hire a chimpanzee to string them together at random, and you will come up with a typical opening paragraph from any 1993 issue of any newsmagazine in America: slackers, whiners, twentysomethings, national debt, Social Security, *The Brady Bunch, Star Wars*, shrinking opportunities, grunge, Seattle, coffeehouse, Wendy Kopp, Lead or Leave, zines, purple hair, tattoos, piercings, TV, Prozac, Lollapalooza, disenfranchised, Elizabeth Wurtzel, *Doc Martens* . . .

Let's stop now.

Looking at those words doesn't bring back a memory of being young in the nineties as much as it brings back the sluggish, dispiriting sensation of *reading articles* about being young in the nineties.

So, fine, the terminology is problematic. At the same time, why pretend that we have any other options? Can we move on now?

X

Before we do, though, is it worth asking whether or not a generation even exists? Can any one thread be said to unify a group of people who were born at the same time, or is that merely a convenient and romantic fiction?

The idea of a generation had enough ballast for Ernest Hemingway, who in 1926 chose Gertrude Stein's quip "You are all a lost generation" as one of the two epigraphs to *The Sun Also Rises*. The other curtain-opener comes from the book of Ecclesiastes: "One generation passeth away, and another generation cometh; but the earth abideth forever." Which seems to suggest that this generation thing hath been with us for a while.

When, in 1956, Allen Ginsberg unleashed his most famous poem, *Howl*, with the opening line "I saw the best minds of my generation destroyed by madness, starving hysterical naked," I suppose a logical response from one of his fully clothed contemporaries might have been, "Hey, Al, I really think that's overstating it. Here we are living in Parsippany, my wife Judy and I, and we're faring just fine. The icebox is stocked to the gills, the kids are healthy and loving school, it's a beautiful day, and I'm teeing off at the Brookhaven Club right after lunch." There were plenty of Americans in the 1920s who were not lost, just as there were plenty in the 1950s who were not beat.

The lost generation, the beat generation, even the silent generation—these terms were always meant to describe faint eddies of resistance along the great gushing river of mass culture.

When Joan Didion published *The White Album* at the end of the seventies, she saw fit to include an essay called "On the Morning After the Sixties." In it Didion, counting herself among the silents, described a sensibility in which I suspect more than a few Xers can hear a few familiar chimes. "We were silent because the exhilaration of social action seemed to many of us just one more way of escaping the personal, of masking for a while that dread of the meaningless which was man's fate," she writes. "To have assumed that particular fate so early was the peculiarity of my generation. I think now that we were the last generation to identify with adults." Maybe the idea of a generation is a mere contrivance, but it's a contrivance that delivers a fair amount of comfort, and even some sense of order, to those who play along.

But okay, fine, if Ecclesiastes and Ginsberg and Joan Didion don't do it for you, there are always the sages of the advertising business. In 1999, Volkswagen released a TV commercial for a convertible called the Cabrio. In the ad, four sensitive, artsy-but-sporty souls are driving to a house party. They weave along empty roads, hands and hair drifting in the night air, the lamp of our lunar satellite hanging above, while "Pink Moon," a ballad by the doomed and fragile seventies folksinger Nick Drake, wisps along in the background. They get to the party. The party appears to suck. They see a frat boy, arms upraised, emitting a halfhearted "whooo!" They know, instinctively, what entering this party will entail, that it will harsh the buzz of whatever back-road reverie the Volkswagen Cabrio has allowed them to enjoy. And so they turn around—they skip the party altogether and rumble onto the road for a few more hours of Nick Drake and moonlight.

Dismiss them as consumerist slime if you wish, but those advertising people knew what they were doing. Not only did they recognize that Nick Drake was in the process of being rescued from obscurity, but they understood that when it came to the target buyer of the Volkswagen Cabrio, nothing flooded his or her heart with a more jubilant ache than the thought of a forgotten talent getting a flush of recognition. Armed, no doubt, with polling data and meticulous spreadsheets and covert squadrons of black-ops Brooklyn cool hunters, the advertising people must have sensed, too, that a sea change was under way. It cannot be an accident that the Cabrio commercial debuted in 1999, because 1999 was the year in which Xers, as a cultural force, truly began to bypass the party. If the mantle of contemporary adulthood descends at that moment when you figure out that MTV doesn't love you anymore, then you can pinpoint the end of our protracted adolescence to 1999. That was the year when Britney Spears materialized in a plaid miniskirt at the top of the pop charts, and it was the year in which the tuneless white-rap *Einsatzgruppen* known as Limp Bizkit helped turn Woodstock III into a heaving melee of rape and arson. It was the year of the Columbine killings—I remember seeing the news reports while my wife and I were on our honeymoon—and it was the year when the stock market became so absurdly overheated that companies hawking underwear and dog food on their Web sites thought it made sense to sell shares of their stock for $437 a pop. By 1999 a fecal tide of suckitude, suckness, and suckronicity was upon us, and the only sensible reaction, the reaction that I happen to think reflects a generational belief system, was to back out the car, bag the party, and get the hell out of Dodge.

That summer, in the *Village Voice*, Eric Weisbard wistfully lamented the passing:

> Nirvana sold a few records in 1992, Clinton was elected, and the rotation seemed complete: boomers assumed political power and we post-everythings were going to

inherit the counterculture or, better yet, steer the consumer culture. Finally: we were already well into our twenties. Yes, there was groaning as underground went mainstream—that's part of the drill. But admit it, my fellow Neverminders, it was a kick seeing our own ilk mopping up all the attention. . . .

In a blink it was gone. Hordes of *Star Search*, Menudo, and the new Mickey Mouse Club alumni were given every-thing, just as the '60s dinosaurs were. We'd always been Born Too Late. Suddenly we were Born Too Early as well.

A strangeness descended—a shift in American consciousness that had to be attributed to more than "we're just getting old." All of a sudden loving Sonic Youth and being baffled by Britney Spears made you a hopeless square. All of a sudden believing in the spirit of an oppositional subculture turned you into a fossil. For his labors, Weisbard received a gladiatorial lashing in the public arena, but he was by no means the first mortician to inspect the pale cor-pus. In fact, Douglas Coupland himself had announced the expira-tion of the generation all the way back in 1995 in *Details*:

> And now I'm here to say that X is over. I'd like to declare a moratorium on all the noise, because the notion that there now exists a different generation—X, Y, K, whatever—is no longer debatable. Kurt Cobain's in heaven, *Slacker*'s at Blockbuster, and the media refers to anyone aged thirteen to thirty-nine as Xers. Which is only further proof that mar-keters and journalists never understood that X is a term that defines not a chronological age but a way of looking at the world.

Whatever the date of departure, it's probably good that we left when we did, because by now America has arrived—thanks again, Mr. Warhol—at the quintessential pomo-trash moment. The new national mantra is: *everything is okay*. Whatever floats across the radar screen, whether it's a botched war or televised karaoke, we are meant to greet it—all of us, as patriotic Americans—with a knowing laugh and an indifferent gaze. Consider the emptied-out flask of Paris Hilton's whispery voice—*that's hot, that's hot*—and think of the way Warhol, a master of the same marzipan-faced mode of spectral-mannequin deadness, was known for reacting to everything that crossed his field of vision with a kind of listless antienthusiasm: *wow, great, great, wow*. And imagine what camp fun Andy would have had at 11:15 in the morning on the day after the fifth anniversary of the September 11 attacks, when these were the headlines on the home page of America Online:

THE STARS ARE READY TO DANCE: WILL JERRY SPRINGER
OR TUCKER CARLSON SWEEP US OFF OUR FEET?

———

20 JOBS WITH HIGHEST STARTING PAY

———

HOW TO SPOT DESIGNER KNOCKOFFS

———

EYELESS MAN ARRESTED FOR DRIVING

———

MARINES SEE GRIM OUTLOOK FOR WESTERN IRAQ

———

MOST FABULOUS AUTOMOBILES OF 2006

———

STINGRAYS KILLED IN REVENGE FOR STEVE IRWIN'S DEATH?

———

WORLD'S BEST AIR GUITARIST CROWNED

———

BEYONCE'S $1 MILLION B-DAY PRESENT

So, what interests me, and what presumably interests you if you've picked up this book, is what comes next?

X

I've provided only half of the definition of *athazagoraphobia*. It's got two meanings.

Athazagoraphobia signifies not only the fear of being forgotten, but the fear of forgetting. It refers to the apprehension that one of these days you're going to wake up and, like the groping protagonists in *Memento* and *The Matrix*, suffer from a strain of amnesia that will blot out crucial elements of your identity. This is the other shoe. Let's listen to it drop.

It happens—the forgetting. We get older. We lose our bearings. We lose track of what we wanted to accomplish and which compromises we wouldn't accept. Responsibilities mount, and nice yuppie things suddenly grow so much nicer. Money—the need for it—nags at us in ways we didn't expect. Even if you wanted to rev yourself up with some "visionary" mode of thinking, doing so just feels ludicrous in the middle of one of those afternoons when you're freaking out about the broken headlight and the preschool bill and the unforeseen illness that the insurance company doesn't cover, and "outsider status" seems like a logical concept until you realize that rigidly maintaining it might leave you unable to pay for medical treatment for your kid. It's an obvious point, but the album cover of Nirvana's *Nevermind* still captures the ambivalence about status that our generation has been forced to come to terms with, one way or another: there's a baby submerged in a pool, and in front of him floats a dollar bill on a fish hook.

We're yuppies now. To paraphrase Allen Ginsberg, I've seen the best minds of my generation riding the Napa Valley Wine Train, setting up Big Meetings, tapping away at their Trēos, racking up the frequent-flier miles, swooning over Fantastic Spicy Elvis rolls, and pretending to care very deeply about the global marketing of some new wireless wonder widget that nobody will ever need. I'm no different. Years ago, when I was happy to get a night's sleep on a hay bale in a Moroccan olive grove, I never expected to wake up a couple of decades later and care as much as I now do about extra-virgin olive oil.

Forgetting is what Americans do. But as long as our amnesia is not too severe, I suspect that dropping out of the limelight might be the loveliest stroke of good fortune that has befallen Generation X since the release of the first Smiths album. We were never cut out for the glare in the first place, and whenever it has been aimed at one of our daisy-in-a-pavement-crack revolutions, the revolution has shriveled up like some rare Peruvian cave fungus that dies when it's exposed to sunlight. To seek the *rise up!* adrenaline rush of a revolution is to overburden ourselves with false hope. We know it never works out.

The boomers got their money and blew it. We have a chance now, as yuppies, or just as *adults*, to cull whatever capital, influence, and media savvy we've amassed and to use it for good. That doesn't mean there is any point in trying to start a "movement," at least not one so visible and self-congratulatory that it curls up as soon as somebody trains a camera on it. The expatriate scene in Prague in the early 1990s, grunge, indie film and indie rock, the dot-com gold rush—all these cultural blips were portrayed in the press as revolutions that never quite panned out. (Or, in the case of the dot-coms, a revolution that unraveled in a flurry of huckster greed.) Even if great things emerged from each of those vagabond leaps in attention, we know that the chasing of chic insurrections and "paradigm shifts" has a tendency to lead to disillusionment.

The boomers, upon reaching this point of understanding, decided to give up. *Hey, amigo, if America can't be a big, stoned, free-love carnival where there's peace between all the brothers and sisters and every roof shines with solar panels and "Purple Haze" becomes the national anthem, then forget it. I'm just going to go into marketing for Union Carbide and buy myself a five-ton Hummer and a chardonnay McMansion down by the bay—one with a cookspace just like the amaaazing kitchen in that Diane Keaton movie, you know, the one where she's still so sexy that both Jack Nicholson and Keanu Reeves can't keep their hands off her!*

Generation X can do better than that, and can do better precisely *because* we're cynical about a phrase like "change the world." One of the more memorable pieces of business jargon from the dot-com frenzy was the term *stealth mode*, which was used to describe a company that had masked itself in secrecy—sometimes even using tricks that seemed to come straight out of *Espionage for Dummies*—in order to fool and outmaneuver its competitors. While I concede that it's blatantly hypocritical for me to be saying this in a book, it needs nevertheless to be said: the way for Generation X to survive—as a philosophy, as an antidote to the Gumpian buffoonery of American culture—is to go into stealth mode. Maybe then we can get something done.

In spite of what we've been trained to think, Generation X has done a lot already. The more the boomers talk about bringing the world together, the less they succeed at it, but a thousand Woodstocks couldn't touch what Generation X has already accomplished through the shrewd and inspired use of media and technology. In the pages ahead I hope to look back at some of the high and low points in the Gen-X odyssey, to introduce the reader to a few people embarking on their own private missions and mutinies, and to provide whatever I can in the way of exhortation or solace for anyone who's thinking about doing the same.

Way back in the eighties, Bret Easton Ellis opened his first novel, *Less Than Zero*, with a line from a great Los Angeles band named, fortuitously, X. The song was "The Have-Nots." The line was "This is the game that moves as you play." That, two decades later, is what Xers have to contend with: a playing field that has not only shifted beyond recognition but has also taken on shifting as its very business model. Back during the merciless job interviews you sat through after you'd left college, your superiors told you to hunker down and pay your dues, so it feels like a slap in the face to spend fifteen or twenty years hunkering down and paying your dues only to discover, at the end of your apprenticeship, that *paying dues itself* is now seen as weak, geezery, even suspect.

This collective bait and switch isn't confined to pop culture. If you're in any line of business, from General Motors to Merrill Lynch to Time Warner, and you're teetering anywhere near the neighborhood of forty, you stand in a perilous place, because you know how to do the old stuff really well—maybe as well as anybody ever could—but nobody seems to give a shit about the old stuff anymore. And this new stuff? You could do it well, too—you're flexible—if you could only figure out what it *is*. Because sometimes it looks like selling air.

Let's not kid ourselves. This is a manifesto for a generation that's never had much use for manifestos. I'm putting it out there anyway because I think it's a fruitful time to take stock of the things Generation X has accomplished—I mean, before we all get really old and start studying our bowel movements—and because I think the Grand Guignol suckiness of the Bush years has left a lot of people, not just Gen Xers, feeling restless, cranky, and famished for change. My own distaste for the grand statement means that I get a spurt of acid reflux whenever I attempt to say something like "It's time for this generation to reclaim the passion that drove it in the first place," but what's reassuring is that a lot of Xers discreetly, tentatively feel the same way. They're just as wary and skeptical as they've been rumored to be, and yet they are in fact (*gag . . . grumble . . . wince*) changing the world. Right now. No joke. They've envisioned the kind of country that they'd like to see, and they're acting in ways that will help bring it about. They are, in their muted way, trying to keep America from sucking.

Viewed from the outside, fine, let people think we're an army of yupster antique dealers, puttering around in granny glasses and moth-eaten cardigans, fishing through a milk crate for that pristine vinyl copy of *Daydream Nation* while everybody else rushes home for the Clay Aiken Thanksgiving special. We know what's really going on. We're the ones lying in wait like a parking lot full of Trojan horses.

X SAVES THE WORLD

QUICK FIRST-PERSON TANGENT: CELEBRATED SUMMER 1984

We are pathetic. We are stars.

—*Dave Eggers,* A Heartbreaking Work of Staggering Genius

It's 1984 and I'm spending the summer scooping ice cream for tourists in Laguna Beach, California. This is exactly two decades before the town will cease to be a town and will, instead, become a reality show on MTV. I've just graduated from high school, and even though the French gentleman who owns the ice cream store is aware of this fact and what it tends to imply in the way of personal responsibility, he insists on making a rash business decision: he gives me and Phil, my eighteen-year-old comrade in the art of the waffle cone, complete control of the sound system.

The sound system is piped into a public patio where Forest Avenue and the South Coast Highway meet. Which means that Phil and I have been handpicked by this generous Gaul to provide the subliminal soundtrack for thousands of international visitors as they pass through the heart of our whimsical seaside village. In fact, we are just a few feet from Laguna's famous Greeter's Corner, where for many years an old bearded gent who looks like an ancient mariner from a box of frozen fish sticks has been recruited to stand all day long in the scalding sun, waving at cars and confused pedestrians. He is the greeter. Most people assume that the greeter is homeless, and therefore they steer clear of him. This, of course, only makes the greeter more aggressive about greeting people.

Phil and I see ourselves as greeters, too, and we're wondering how far we can push it. It turns out that we can push it very far. Most of the time the sound system at the ice cream store is tuned to K-EARTH 101, the Los Angeles oldies station, but there's a cassette player in the back where the French guy bakes the croissants every morning. Phil and I decide to bring in some tapes. We see this as a sociological experiment; sort of like that test they did at Yale where the scientist asked people to zap other people with jolts of electricity. What we're wondering is, *What kind of music will prove so intolerable to the tourists that they will find it impossible to enjoy their croissants and waffle cones?*

We start out with Elvis Costello, having determined that albums like *This Year's Model* and *Imperial Bedroom* sound sober and pleasant enough that nobody will notice that they are not listening to the Beach Boys. We are correct. Elvis Costello produces no discernible change in behavior among the tourists on the patio. Satisfied customers buy their waffle cones, eat them, and leave without a word. *Hmmm.* Phil and I upgrade to Echo & the Bunnymen: surely Ian McCulloch, gas-baggily crooning about the killing moon, will shoo away the Motown-loving day-trippers in droves. But no, nothing happens. Waffle cone sales remain brisk, and not even the Frenchman complains about our patio soundtrack—a phenomenon that we attribute to the profound Frenchiness of Echo & the Bunnymen. Well then, how about the Smiths? Can a brood of pasty, sun-burned Christians from Nebraska really stand there ordering their triple-decker Rocky Road and Bubble Gum ziggurats without once doing a double take at colossally gay lyrics like "You can pin and mount me like a butterfly"? Yes, it turns out they can. We sell as much ice cream as ever, and we seem to get even busier when we up the ante with Grandmaster Flash & The Furious Five. How can this be? How can someone listen to these unflinching narratives of inner-city despair and still want sprinkles on top?

Since nothing, so far, has been able to dissuade people from clamoring for the Frenchman's waffle cones, Phil and I decide it is time for the nuclear option. It is time to release the Dead Kennedys—specifically an album called *Fresh Fruit for Rotting Vegetables*, a collection of songs with some of the most satirically offensive lyrics ever written. *Someone* is bound to notice, right? Someone sitting in the patio licking a tower of Butter Pecan is bound to come storming into the store, furious about having his Pacific Coast ice cream idyll ruined by lyrics about killing the poor, lynching the landlord, and celebrating holidays in Cambodia.

But no, we never hear a peep. Phil and I learn a useful lesson that summer. Our Greeter's Corner Punk Experiment teaches us something—something that will guide my navigation of the American culture wars for years to come: nothing is more powerful than ice cream.

1. IN BLOOM
1991–1999: RISE + FALL

Watching three movies a day and reading doesn't sound productive, but it got me here.

—Richard Linklater, *interviewed in* Newsday, *June 29, 1991*

Everybody's coming home for lunch these days . . .

—Camper Van Beethoven, *"Take the Skinheads Bowling"*

Can you feel it? You must *feel* the anticipation.

It is the fall of 1991, and you're young and single and down to your last few hundred bucks, and you've been driving along a California highway with the windows of the Honda Accord rolled down and the night air streaming in. Now you've parked the car and picked up your ticket at the "will call" booth. Now you're sliding into a seat somewhere in the hull of an immense spaceship. The spaceship is a major West Coast concert arena. The occupants of the ship are male, for the most part, and they wear facial expressions that speak of both merriment and solemnity. This is an event. This is a convocation. These men and sporadic women have come to partake of that most ritualized of American sacraments: the rock concert. In 1991 the rock concert is only about twenty-five years old, and yet everyone in attendance can be forgiven for thinking that its ceremonial rites have been around for centuries—since the signing of the Magna Carta, maybe, or since the Sumerians sank their sandals into the rich silt of the Tigris and the Euphrates. You *know what to do* at a rock concert. We all do. The young men milling around the deck of the spaceship understand precisely what will happen during the next couple of hours, and there is in that knowledge as much comfort as there is release. They will wait for the moment when the house lights flick off, and then, with that cue—*waaaaaaahhhhh*—they will go uniformly apeshit.

Look, here it comes now: the blackening of the room, the surge of chesty whooping from the crowd, the arms shooting into the air, the sardonic raising of cigarette lighters, the tiny airport lights blinking red and blue from the lip of the stage, the local radio guy grabbing the microphone and asking rhetorical questions regarding the crowd's readiness to rock, the way he finally bellows out the announcement with a kind of horror-movie zeal: "Ladies and gentlemen, the biggest-selling rock-and-roll band from the great rock-and-roll city of Seattle, Washington . . . QUEENSRŸCHE!!!"

X

You were, perhaps, expecting someone else?

I know, but please bear with me as we make a brief detour in the interest of context. The Generation X thing is about to explode, yes—Nirvana, *Slacker*, Douglas Coupland!—but perhaps it's useful to remember what it felt like in the United States of America moments before that happened.

In 1991 I was unemployed. That was a pretty common experience in those days. If you happened to graduate from college after the stock market crash of 1987, there's a good chance that you spent a fair amount of your time going from one job interview to another, and it was during those interviews that you began hearing about hiring freezes and cutbacks, downsizing and shrinking industries—*so sorry* and *truly sorry* and *we just don't have any openings right now*—and after each interview you would invariably crawl back to your mousehole of an apartment (or, worse, mom and dad's house) and repeat the phrase "What am I going to do with my life?" like some kind of psychotic mantra.

Faced with this turn of events, a lot of sensible people scurried back to the relative security of grad school. I, less sensibly, did not. While working as a political reporter in North Carolina, I'd seen some footage of Czechoslovakia's Velvet Revolution happening on CNN, and that had been enough to inspire me to liquidate my puny bank account and join the first wave of American expatriates in Prague. The fall of Communism! It was a time of action, of change, of watching the world wake up from history, as that dude from Jesus Jones would put it. It was . . . *something to do other than sitting around at home watching Jesus Jones videos*. I caught a cheap flight to Prague—as did a lot of other young Americans, it turned out—where at night I passionately committed every penny of my dwindling bank account to fostering free speech and democracy within the city's tight-knit community of beer drinkers and bartenders, and where during the day I spent a substantial amount of time absorbing the impact of this huge historical event while lounging on the steps of the Jan Hus Monument, in the middle of the Old Town Square, and watching a medieval astronomical clock. The clock loomed above the square. There was a skeleton on the right side of it—one of those beguiling European curios that call to mind a time of traveling minstrels, blood-soaked meat markets, scythe-wielding emissaries of death, and bubonic plague. Every hour the skeleton would grab a rope with his bony fingers and toll a bell. Usually around noon I would get a hot dog.

A few months later I wound up back in California—big surprise—where, after fruitless weeks of sending out my résumé and becoming fluent in the language of hiring freezes and shrinking industries, I somehow persuaded an Orange County newspaper to use me as a freelance rock critic. In this role I probably earned about $500 total for the year, and, to add to that humiliation, my status as the paper's heavy-metal benchwarmer meant that I got stuck with the ridiculous concerts that nobody on staff wanted to cover. The most memorable of these ridiculous concerts was Queensrÿche's.

Queensrÿche specialized in a bastard fusion of hair metal and prog rock. They had a concept album out called *Operation: Mindcrime*, which had a message about an evil Orwellian state and brainwashing and the power of the individual—something like that. I don't remember a single melody from *Operation: Mindcrime*. They had another album, too—a new one, called *Empire*—which had foisted upon the American airwaves a song with arguably the most hilarious title in recorded history: "Silent Lucidity." If you want to get a sense of what Queensrÿche sounded like, and what Nirvana and Generation X were up against, imagine *Aaron Spelling Presents Pink Floyd's "The Wall"* with a revised libretto by Rod McKuen. In other words, this was the sort of act that saw no shame in recording a song called "Silent Lucidity." I have nothing against either silence or lucidity, mind you, and in fact I can see how silence and lucidity, in tandem, could play a useful role in the ongoing process of one's personal development. But *come on*.

Queenrÿche billed themselves, around the fall of 1991, as the biggest-selling band from Seattle. Which was a hoot, because I'd already seen the video for a song called "Smells Like Teen Spirit"— a song that every unemployed college grad in America would greet, for some inchoate reason, as if it were manna from heaven—and I knew Queensrÿche were doomed. You could feel it. That spaceship may have been packed, but you could smell the waft of spent laser fumes in the air. *Your days are numbered, Queensrÿche! Ha, ha, ha, ha-ha! Soon Nirvana will rise up and crush you like a worm!*

The World Is Yours: All Rise for the Cooler King

Even though there is something inherently phony and bankrupt about memorializing big moments in pop culture, we can't get around it here: the debut of Nirvana's "Smells Like Teen Spirit" video will always loom large in the Gen-X brainpan. Here's where the Xers take over—fleetingly, yes, but indisputably. Here's where we grab the pitchforks and storm the Bastille. I remember it clearly, and it *did* seem to happen to me or to some pent-up configuration of "us." Kurt Cobain had encoded it right there in the lyrics of the song: "our little group." What was the little group? Who was in it? You couldn't be sure, although in my mind, at least, the group knew something about cutbacks and hiring freezes and something about the absurdity of a song called "Silent Lucidity."

If the history of pop is shaped like a parabola, the largely forgotten lacuna at the end of the eighties and the very beginning of the nineties has to qualify as a precipitous dip in the loop. You might compare it to the Soviet Union in the sleepy years between Brezhnev and Gorbachev, when blah bureaucratic placeholders like Yuri Andropov and Konstantin Chernenko each vaguely "ruled" for a few months at a time. You could find compelling music around 1990 or so—yes, of course. Public Enemy was still on fire, N.W.A.'s *Straight Outta Compton* had gangsterized hip-hop, the perpetually aggrieved and penitentially shorn Irish songbird Sinéad O'Connor had become a strange and unlikely media star, and a gummy, prickly new strain of garage rock was starting to howl its way out of the Pacific Northwest. Even so, pop suffered from what you might call a leadership vacuum. Prince and R.E.M. and Guns N' Roses obliged the radio with hits, but the most fervent of their acolytes muttered that their most vital work was behind them. (In R.E.M.'s case this turned out to be untrue, but that's how it felt.) For all their promise and pickled swagger, the Replacements had petered out before ever making it to the cocktail party. Mary J. Blige was still just a background singer for Uptown. The Pixies spent their time chewing over the frustration of having released a masterpiece, *Doolittle*, that the mainstream seemed determined to ignore. Into this vacuum—into this somnolently wide-open period of sitting around waiting—rushed some of the lamest and most negligible acts you'd ever be forced to listen to. Even if you were *not* prone to be a snob about the "tacky" genres—teen pop and disco, hair metal and power ballads—you would have a hard time finding anything ironically positive or even snidely amusing to say about Color Me Badd and the New Kids on the Block, Richard Marx and the C+C Music Factory, Tesla and Cinderella and Warrant. The problem with this music wasn't that it was tacky, per se. The problem was that it sounded criminally generic and boring—it was manufactured sonic data that'd had the lifeblood leeched out of it. The other problem was that it was everywhere. This was, shall we say, a highly pernicious time to be stuck at home watching a lot of MTV.

In those days MTV was kind enough to maintain a little barrio for the folks who didn't necessarily *need* to see Color Me Badd's "I Wanna Sex You Up" or Warrant's "Cherry Pie" one more time. The barrio was called *120 Minutes*. It aired late on Sunday nights, and it's where the little group went, presumably after a week of clown-costumed toil in the service sector, to glut itself on Nine Inch Nails and My Bloody Valentine, the Cure and the Cocteau Twins, the Stone Roses and the Pogues. Many of these bands had nothing in common except that they were herded together as "alternative." That's *alternative* with a lowercase *a*. The word had not yet grown horns and a forked tail. It had not yet become a term of art in the field of global marketing. "Alternative" simply meant something you couldn't find anywhere else. Calling a band alternative was the kiss of death if you wanted to sell any records.

And yet . . . just that summer Perry Farrell, a sleazy-shamanic Pacific Coast scamp who might have been cooked up by Joan Didion and Carlos Castaneda after a midnight screening of *Blade Runner*, had brought these scattered tribes together for the first Lollapalooza tour. If you bought a ticket to Lollapalooza you got to see some combination of Fishbone, Ice T, Nine Inch Nails, the Butthole Surfers, Siouxsie and the Banshees, Henry Rollins, the Violent Femmes, Living Colour, and Farrell's own band of thundering miscreants, Jane's Addiction. Somehow, Lollapalooza had turned into something big. Here the "alternative" wasn't supposed to make any money and all of a sudden swarms of people were lining up for it. Maybe they'd been hungry all along, but nobody had thought of trying to bring them together. Buying the alternative in 1991 was like voting for Democrats in 1991. You'd gotten so accustomed to losing that you had internalized the expectation of failure.

X

So I turn on *120 Minutes* one Sunday night and there sits Dave Kendall, the host of the show. I hear a high-pitched buzzing sound and I see a frenzied montage of insects—beetles, butterflies, caterpillars (that's how the show always starts), and then Kendall, who is British, announces the debut of Nirvana's "Smells Like Teen Spirit."

The song begins. *F sus4. B-flat. A-flat sus4. D-flat.*

The opening note clusters of the song sound as though they are being strummed in a padded cell on a guitar whose strings have been warped by a few hairbreadths. The chords are followed by a thump of percussion that seems to drop from the sky like a Brobdingnagian medicine ball . . .

KOOPF KOOPF KOOPF KOOPF

This is followed by a sequence of garage-rock power chords that manage to burrow laparoscopically into whatever parts of the human brain regulate decision making, the control of your limbs, and a propensity for grunting and drooling. They're like the chords in "Louie Louie" or "Billie Jean" or "London Calling"—primal chords, Pavlovian chords. Resistance is futile.

Now I am no longer on the couch. I am alone in the house but I don't want to sit. I walk right up to the television, to the screen itself, and I see this scoliotic blond guy in a green-and-brown-striped Charlie Brown T-shirt lurching back and forth and staring right back at me with a look of . . . what is it? Joy? Wrath? Contempt?

> *Hello, hello, hallo, how low?*
> *Hello, hello, hallo, how low?*

Hello, Kurt.

The drummer is Cousin It on a Jolt bender. The bass player is Paul Bunyanesque—a tottering timberland giant. The band is playing in a high school gymnasium where there are cheerleaders in black leotards with the red anarchy symbol stitched into the front. The cheerleaders are pumping their pom-poms back and forth in slo-mo, and the song seems to be rushing forward on a thousand black hooves, and the crowd up there in the gymnasium bleachers—*holy shit*, the kids are scattering now, just piling down from the bleachers and surrounding the band in an adrenal vortex of leaps and crashes and collisions. The kids refuse to adhere to the rules of rock performance conduct as laid out in 1949 by the Geneva Convention. This is not a Queensrÿche show. They are not going *predictably* apeshit. They are going *genuinely* apeshit, and everything is coming apart at the seams.

> *Here we are now*
> *Entertain us*

Here we are now. Exactly. Thank you.

Perhaps you believe that rock videos qualify as the most pointless and bovine of all modern diversions—in which case I congratulate you on your perspicacity, Mr. Brooks—but this is without question the greatest rock video ever made. There is not a false moment. There is not a bad frame—okay, the janitor swaying back and forth to the beat with his slop mop, *that's* ludicrous, but still. I want to see this video again, right away. I want to hear the song. I want to eat the song for breakfast. I want to butter my toast with this song. I want to floss my teeth with this song. I want to gas up the Accord with this song. I want to inflict this song on the tourists buying ice cream down at the Greeter's Corner. Up until this moment I have been vaguely aware of Nirvana and some larval "rock scene" up in the Pacific Northwest. Strangely, I even own a copy of the band's first album, *Bleach*, on pink collectible vinyl, although I can't say that it has roused in me any sense of urgency. But *this*—

This is the sound of a generation setting aside its ambivalence, for once. This is no fluke. This is the sound of success. The song purrs with ambition. You don't record a song like this if you want to be ignored. It's monstrous, yeah, but it's *pretty,* too. In the quiet parts the delicate harmonics pealing off of Cobain's metal strings sound like Tibetan wind chimes. The song is like a birthday cake that's been baked with layers and layers of fudgy, gritty sediment at the bottom, but on top the baker has smeared a sweet layer of pink and blue frosting.

You figure it out in sixty seconds: "Smells Like Teen Spirit" is a Cooler King moment.

Cooler King Hilts is the character played by Steve McQueen in the 1963 film *The Great Escape.* He's an inmate in a high-security, concertina-wired Nazi POW camp during World War II, but no matter where the Nazis put him, no matter how tightly the Krauts lock him down, the Cooler King keeps finding ways to break free. Stoic, defiant, as unsinkable as a buoy, McQueen treats his incarceration the way a twelve-year-old geek might treat the latest installment of Final Fantasy—as a puzzle to be gamed out through persistence and pluck. In the most famous scene from *The Great Escape,* Cooler King hops onto a Triumph TR6 Trophy motorcycle, skids it around to pick up momentum, hits a ramp, and sails right over the fence of the camp. He goes racing through a pastoral alpine landscape straight out of *The Sound of Music*—green fields, snowcapped mountains—until, of course, he gets tangled like a trout in the wires the Germans have laid out near the Swiss border. Back to the camp he goes—but not without having sucked in the clear air of freedom, at least for a few hours. In *that* lies his victory. He's caught, but indomitable. The other, weaker prisoners can't help but take inspiration from that.

American pop culture is a parade of endless tranquilizing banality punctured by these Cooler King moments, which are very rare. Massive media companies are set up to maximize profits, not to worry about art—art tends to get in the way—but every now and then something springboards over the corporate concertina wire and gives the rest of us, at least for a fleeting instant, the vicarious charge of defiance.

So I'm watching Nirvana and that's what I see. I see Steve McQueen gunning a Triumph through the Schwarzwald. I see Iggy Pop dancing like a spastic chimp on *The Dinah Shore Show*. I see Sylvia Plath reading "Daddy" aloud to a prim, gasping auditorium. I see somebody getting away—and getting away with it. Just when you think *the things that are not supposed to happen* are never going to happen anymore, they do.

The next day I drive into town. I head for a record store called Sound Spectrum, where I make a beeline for the *N* section and find Randy Newman, the New York Dolls, Nine Inch Nails, the Nitty Gritty Dirt Band, Orchestral Manoeuvres in the Dark.

No Nirvana. Could Geffen Records have botched the distribution so badly that copies of *Nevermind* are now impossible to track down? You get used to watching one band after another succumb to the perfectly timed gaffe. You expect them to collapse in the face of the yawning indifference of the masses. *Remember what happened to the Replacements?* I see, I get it—*foiled again*. Just when we find a band that's truly on the precipice of greatness, some corporate *glitch* manages to interfere and . . .

"Uh, hey," I ask the beardy poo-bah at the cash register. "I'm looking for an album by this band called Nirvana."

"You, too, eh?"

"What?"

"You're like the twentieth person to come in here and ask me about that."

"I am?"

"Yeah."

"Huh."

"Yeah. We're all out."

"You're sold out of it? Already?"

"Yep."

"Huh."

"Actually, I think we've still got one on cassette . . ."

Breed

I want a tie-dyed shirt made with the blood of Jerry Garcia.

—*Kurt Cobain, in* Heavier Than Heaven, *a biography by Charles R. Cross*

Even though it succeeded in delivering a Cooler King moment, there was nothing explicitly revolutionary about *Nevermind*. It's not as though Cobain wrote protest songs. Just imagine the frustration over at Rock the Vote as the interns sifted through pages and pages of Nirvana lyrics looking for slogans that could be used to mobilize the masses—only to come up with "stay away" and "sell the kids for food."

In spite of his transparent ambition, Cobain was a conflicted and classically tortured artist, and he didn't parade around declaring, *Beware! We are soldiers of grunge and we shall overthrow the established order!* Other people—critics and fans—said such things, but Cobain himself tended to be skeptical about moony utopian dreaming, and he put up as much shifty resistance as he could. "I just felt that my band was in a situation where it was expected to fight in a revolutionary sense toward the major corporate machine," he told Michael Azerrad in *Come as You Are: The Story of Nirvana.* "It was expected by a lot of people. A lot of people just flat out told me that 'You can really use this as a tool. You can use this as something that will really change the world.' I just thought, 'How dare you put that kind of fucking pressure on me. It's stupid. And I feel stupid and contagious.' " A song like "Smells Like Teen Spirit" was, as Azerrad observed, "a sarcastic reaction to the idea of actually having a revolution, yet it also embraces the idea." That duality, that stuckness between a desire for change and profound doubts about how to achieve it, would come to define the philosophy of X. If the boomers had shot their wad by trying to forge a utopia, Kurt Cobain was saving the world by steering his generation away from that delusion.

The Velvet Revolution, which had brought democracy and free speech to Czechoslovakia two years earlier, and which had gotten thousands of American Xers flustered enough to hop a plane to Europe, had floated up from a world of muffled dissent and strategic surrealism. In a similar way, *Nevermind* would exert its mutinous influence on the pop charts, and on the national psyche, in more bizarre and subtle ways than anyone expected. To listen to *Nevermind* now is to marvel at both its pulverizing atomic firepower and its bacterial weirdness, its silk and its grime. During the first month of 1992 *Nevermind* enjoyed a decisive symbolic victory by knocking Michael Jackson's *Dangerous* off the top of the *Billboard* album chart, and it's still amazing that once upon a time, a chart-conquering rock album teemed with lyrics as thrillingly cracked as "God is gay, burn the flag" and "Chew your meat for you / Pass it back and forth in a passionate kiss" and "A mulatto / An albino / A mosquito / My libido."

Imagine: that last line was more or less the *chorus* of a big hit single in the United States of America, and yet it seems to owe more of a debt to metaphysical poetry than to Casey Kasem and twofer Tuesdays. If you're looking for anything revolutionary in Nirvana's music, this is where you'll find it, and if you're looking for an antecedent to a couplet like "A mosquito / My libido," you might have to travel all the way back to "The Flea," a poem written by John Donne at the tail end of the sixteenth century:

> *Mee it suck'd first, and now sucks thee,*
> *And in this flea, our two bloods mingled bee*

Like Donne and many of the debauched English bards who came before and after him (if grunge had a godfather, it was undoubtedly

Chaucer), Cobain had a fixation on bodily organs and fluids, on physiology, on stomachs and blood and bile and sour-milk aromas. Reading his lyrics could feel like flipping through a medical textbook. He had a chronic grind in his gut, some excruciating Promethean ulcer that never seemed to heal. Nirvana's next album, *In Utero*, overflowed with this sort of imagery.

> *We feed off each other*
> *We can share our endorphins*
> ("Milk It")

> *Every wet nurse refused to feed him*
> *Electrolytes smell like semen*
> ("Scentless Apprentice")

> *I'm on warm milk and laxatives*
> *Cherry-flavored antacids*
> ("Pennyroyal Tea")

> *Throw down your umbilical noose*
> *So I can climb right back*
> ("Heart-Shaped Box")

If you were a boomer cruising around the Hamptons listening to Eric Clapton's fern-bar blooz in your yellow Lotus Elan, icky-sticky laments like these signified the arrival of a new guard. But for Xers who'd been bonding over the secret history of this music for ten or fifteen years—the Pixies and the Replacements, the Bad Brains and X, Patti Smith and the Cramps—*Nevermind*'s chart conquest felt like the vindication of an old one. Kurt Cobain was the beautiful boy, the emissary, the feral moppet with the boomerang in *The Road Warrior*—the kid who quietly watches the mohawked skirmishes from his gopher hole and then grows up to lead the bedraggled community of survivors.

By 1993 it was, thanks to the moppet, a bright alternative morning. The car radio was alternative—crawling with Breeders and Lemonheads. The TV was alternative—turn it on and you saw Bart Simpson and *Beavis and Butt-Head*. By 1993 a bulletin had gone out, which is exactly why anyone with a sense of history knew it couldn't last. Scientists had located and identified the X pathogen, and they were doing everything they could to keep the alternative epidemic under control. From what I could tell, the experts were employing the same ingenious approach that they'd used on the California fruit flies. See, you can try to gas fruit flies by crop-dusting them with insecticide, but somehow a lot of them manage to survive. This is why scientific authorities conjured up a new plan for the fruit flies. It was called the "sterile insect technique." With the sterile insect technique you'd gather a gigantic swarm of male flies in a laboratory, blast them with chemicals or radiation, and render them infertile. Then you'd release that swarm into the wild. The infertile flies, vastly outnumbering their fertile competition, would mate with as many female flies as they could, and the females would subsequently lay unfertilized eggs. The fruit fly population would plummet. In other words, you flooded an area with *more* fruit flies in order to wind up with less of them.

This was the most sensible way to explain the existence of Stone Temple Pilots. If the major labels flooded the airwaves with "alternative bands" that were in fact sterile, those bands would mate with millions of listeners, and the listeners would quickly decide that "alternative" music sucked as bad as Warrant did, and the infestation would peter out. It wouldn't take long, although the disease control teams *would* have to remain persistent. The Candlebox swarm, the Bush swarm, the Seven Mary Three swarm, the notorious Blind Melon swarm, a swarm that even had its own queen bee—yes, our guardians of national safety had to keep dumping these neutered rock decoys into the ecosphere until the only remnant of the original "alternative" movement was some unshaven gnome listening to Fugazi in a bomb shelter.

Nirvana's alternative ascendancy managed to feel mythic even though, or maybe because, it was doomed to last only three years. Before long it would feel like an actual myth—like something that had never happened. By 2001 Color Me Badd would be back, only now they'd be called 'N Sync. A decade after Cobain killed himself, his widow, Courtney Love, trapped in a maze of crash diets and plastic surgery and tabloid tantrums, would be photographed taking their only child, Frances Bean Cobain, to the taping of a Fox talent show that would not have tolerated ten seconds of "Scentless Apprentice": *American Idol.*

If *Nevermind* changed the world, the world changed back pretty fast. On the other hand, Cobain probably underestimated the power of the virus he'd unleashed. He admitted as much to Azerrad a couple of years after the outbreak of "Smells Like Teen Spirit." "Within the last two years, I've noticed a consciousness that's way more positive, way more intelligent in the younger generation, and the proof is in stupid things like *Sassy* magazine and MTV in general," he said. "Whether you want to admit that or not, there is a positive consciousness and people are becoming more human. I've always been optimistic, but it's the little Johnny Rotten inside me that has to be a sarcastic asshole."

Might

In America, you know, we've got a bug up our butt about something and we just want a change. All right, but what always happens when the change happens is, nothing fuckin' happens. It doesn't change, all right?

—Quentin Tarantino, *in* Newsweek, *December 26, 1994*

New things were happening. Xers tend to be automatically skeptical about Cooler King moments, but factors had converged to create one. *Nevermind* was the most obvious example of what the moment was about, and *Nevermind* soon had plenty of company. There were bikes leaping over the barbed wire. There was a tang of patricidal vengeance in the air. Richard Linklater's *Slacker* had amused and confused audiences at the Sundance Film Festival, Douglas Coupland's *Generation X: Tales for an Accelerated Culture* was going into multiple printings, Dr. Dre and Ice Cube and their comrades in Compton's N.W.A. were forcing M.C. Hammer into early retirement, powerful women like Sinéad O'Connor and Björk and Tori Amos and Mary J. Blige and Liz Phair and Courtney Love were beginning to detonate prim notions of what a woman could say in a pop song, American slack troops were establishing expatriate beachheads in Eastern Europe, scores of new bands were flooding out of (and into) Seattle, Dave Eggers was en route to launching *Might* magazine in San Francisco, the demon seed of reality TV was about to bloom with *The Real World*, high-tech tycoon Michael Dell was about to be named the youngest CEO in the Fortune 500, battalions of computer geeks were creating Web browsers and operating systems and other incomprehensible things in their basements—innovations that would alter the very infrastructure of the global economy and, within a few years, turn many of these fringe dwellers into billionaires.

New things were happening, and the people doing these new things were still in their twenties. (Well, most of them were. Ironically, 1991 was the year in which the two people whose terminology stuck with Gen X like a tattoo, Douglas Coupland and Richard Linklater, were inching conspicuously close to thirty.) Somebody detected it, and overnight a new media narrative was born: Generation X! Judging from the way newspapers and magazines began to pontificate about Generation X, the very idea of a fresh crop of young people came as a shock. Weren't the *boomers* the young people? Isn't that what a young person *was*—a boomer?

"Honey, come here, *look*! It says here that there were *46 million people* born after we were! And my *God*, they don't like the same stuff we do! They never even *saw* the Beatles on *The Ed Sullivan Show. . . ."*

"Oh gosh, snoodles, do you remember where you were when you saw the Beatles on *The Ed Sullivan Show?"*

"Oh boy, do I ever. I think the Beatles changed the world. I really do. I think they *changed the world."*

"They sure did."

Generation X wasn't discovered in 1991 any more than the New World was discovered in 1492. It was . . . noticed. Gen X had been around for a while, all 46 million of us—who else do you think had been reading all those comic books, playing all that Pac-Man, watching all those after-school reruns of *Gilligan's Island* and *Bewitched?* And yet even after Gen X was spotted and given a name, the experts had a hard time figuring out what it was.

The boomers—well, we knew about them. They were born after World War II. With the bloodshed and the Depression finally out of the way, America hopped into bed and passed through a two-decade paroxysm of procreation. The birth rate went vertical all the way through the fifties, and the baby boom dumped into America's lap somewhere north of 70 million kids. It was a generation that could, simply by virtue of its size and the gusher of affluence into which it was born, exert enormous influence over what the country was buying and wearing and listening to and talking about. Little more than a sneeze from a decent cross section of the boomers was enough to thrust just about anything—hula hoops, mood rings, Herman's Hermits—into the spotlight. This led boomers to the conclusion that they could change the world.

Generation X came next, but the experts—after burning through millions of dollars in grant money and toiling away for years in sleepy think tanks—have never been able to agree on when X starts and when it ends. Ask them when all those Generation X people were born, and you will *still* get a variety of dates. Oh, maybe it's 1965–78 or 1960–80 or 1961–81 or 1963–81 or 1960–77. That last example makes the most sense to me, because when I meet people who score high on the GXAT (Generation X Aptitude Test, better known as the G-zat), it usually turns out that they were born between 1960 and 1977. The first question on the GXAT is this:

1. Do you want to change the world?

A Yes, and I'm proud to say we did it, *man*. We *changed the world*. Just look around you!

B Yes, absolutely, and I promise I will get back to doing that just as soon as interest rates return to where they're supposed to be.

C *Omigod, omigod*, changing the world and helping people is, like, *totally* important to me! I worked in a soup kitchen once and it was *so* sad but the poor people there had *so* much dignity!

D The way you phrase that question is so fucking cheesy and absurd that I am not even sure I want to continue with this pointless exercise.

That's the only question on the GXAT. I could tack on a bunch of stuff about John Hughes movies and George Stephanopoulos and the Austrian version of "Rock Me Amadeus," but there is no need. We're done. If you chose *d*, accept it: you're an Xer, even if you happen to be eighty years old. As people like Coupland have been pointing out for years now, X is more a sensibility than a rigidly confined demographic.

That sensibility can be broken down into a lot of different components, but the very concept of "changing the world" presents us with a fine place to start. Over the years I've met plenty of my generational peers who have suffered no shortage of virtues like ambition, drive, boldness, self-sacrifice, and altruism, but I don't recall many of them talking explicitly about changing the world.

They know that if they were to do that, they would set themselves up for a kind of karmic boomerang effect.

We saw it with the previous crew, and we know what happens: as soon as you start blathering about changing the world, *wham*, there you are, squeezed in between Kenny Rogers and Huey Lewis, swaying your hips in the "We Are the World" video. It's not that the world doesn't need changing or that doing so would extract too much strain. It's that talking about it seems to undermine the effort. Why be so obvious about it? Why announce your intentions? Why does changing the world mean that you have to put on your serious face and sing a power ballad with David Hasselhoff? If the boomers were really so committed to sticking it to The Man, why were they always overnighting The Man a memo about it?

This is why the early nineties were both galvanizing and distressing for people who were afflicted with the X sensibility. All of a sudden Xers like Kurt Cobain were changing the world, but they were getting so much attention for it that we knew it would come to a bad end. If anything, the big media discovery of 1991—*Generation X!*—felt a bit like a thirteen-year-old kid kicking over a log and finding, in the patch of wet compost underneath it, a wriggling, squirming colony, a happily self-contained realm of ants and earwigs, pill bugs and earthworms. The thing about the X sensibility that mystified a lot of people was the way the bugs seemed to *prefer* living underneath the log. As if everything had been just fine and dandy until that fucking kid kicked the log away.

Waking Life

"My definition of a slacker is someone who's being responsible to themselves," Richard Linklater told the *Philadelphia Inquirer* in the summer of 1991. "It's not avoiding responsibility; it's finding your own path through this maze of programming and pressures."

After several years of living in Austin and not doing a whole lot, Linklater had finally gotten around to something: he'd shot a

$20,000 movie about living in Austin and not doing a whole lot. The movie was *Slacker*. To this day it remains one of the most eccentric movies ever to attract mainstream attention. Did it "make an impact"? Sort of. It represented the start of an amazing career for Richard Linklater—this is a guy who would go on to direct *Before Sunrise, Before Sunset, Waking Life, Dazed and Confused, Tape, School of Rock*, and *Fast Food Nation*—but it did not represent the start of a movement. Nor did it aspire to. It was not a movie made to be rallied around. To this day you can't attach the usual media shorthand to *Slacker*. Throw words like *prescient* and *influential* at it and they slide right off.

Slacker, like *Eraserhead*, wears its weirdness in a unique and self-contained way. It has ninety-seven characters, not one of whom is crucial to the story line, because of course there is no story line. A camera wanders through Austin, catching glimpses, recording impressions, finally spinning off a cliff. Conspiracy theorists prattle on. Tormented dudes hurl a typewriter into a ravine. People talk about bands they're playing with and bands they've heard about and bands they're going to see that night. A guy sits in a room crammed with blaring TV sets. A woman claims to have in her possession an authentic Madonna Ciccone pap smear. We meet psychics, paranoids, malcontents, anarchists, slogan shouters, arm lickers, shut-ins, and day-trippers. Cultural critic Greil Marcus has used the phrase "the old, weird America" to describe a mythical, precorporate landscape—a nation of drifters and freaks, hucksters and pioneers. Well, if any trace of that old, weird America remained alive in 1991, you could observe it in *Slacker*.

And yet somehow, without being a scheming careerist about it, Linklater had tapped into a widespread phenomenon. Drags on the economy—a narcoleptic Dow, a heels-dug-in recession—had turned the job market into a stagnant pond. In the same way that pop music suffered through a parabolic dip at the end of the eighties, the forces of American enterprise seemed to be stuck in a holding pattern between the preppy *Bonfire of the Vanities* boom of the

Reagan years and the nerdy *Infinite Jest* boom of the Clinton era. Old companies were shearing off costs, and the new companies—the ones up in Seattle and the Silicon Valley that would change the very essence of what a company *was*—remained in embryo. We might call it the Kinko's Lacuna. During the Kinko's Lacuna it was common to spend an unreasonable amount of time at Kinko's copy shops, because you always had to print out extra copies of your résumé, and Kinko's was often the cheapest and easiest place to do it. Hardly anyone used e-mail yet. Your sole option was snail mail, so you accustomed yourself to a routine: send them out, hear nothing in response, print more. (If you were especially enterprising—or, as in my case, bored and broke—you hit the road. In 1991 my friend Rich and I spent a week driving up and down the length of California, stopping in cities like Sacramento and Santa Rosa, trying to meet in person with any potential employer who'd been rash enough to call us back. In Big Sur, Rich slept on a picnic table and I slept in the car. Neither of us got a job out of it.)

Linklater picked up on this. Thanks to their economic predicament, a lot of expensively educated folks *were* spending a lot of time during the Kinko's Lacuna sitting around and talking, which meant that they were hatching a lot of wild-hair ideas, and more than a few of those wild-hair ideas, like *Slacker* itself, were threatening to bubble up into the glare. "There's something about the atmosphere of a university town, the optimistic environment, that feeds the slacker mentality," Linklater said at the time. "It's a phase you go through, and you look back and think, *Oh, God, how ridiculous to sit down and drink coffee and talk all day long*. But I like that. It's a daydream—that's where your breakthroughs come from. To give yourself time to sit around and think. Those years, I was always envisioning my ideal world. And when you don't have any connections to anything, besides just trying to stay alive, your ideal world can be pretty amazing."

This is a crucial point, because what all the newspaper "think pieces" about the slackers failed to point out is that a fair number of slackers were hypersmart. They took great pride in *knowing things* in a way that the millennials, ten or fifteen years later, would not. Even when it looked like the slackers were wasting their time, they weren't. They were learning; they were sponging up information. Two classic examples of this are Quentin Tarantino and Beck. Before Tarantino became his generation's most celebrated filmmaker, he was, as everyone knows, a clerk in a video store, and the way he spent his time in that store, the legendary Video Archives in Manhattan Beach, would play a crucial role in his becoming such a masterful writer and director: he watched movies, thousands of them, all day long. Over time, Tarantino turned himself into a walking Wikipedia of cinematic history—a motormouthed database with carte blanche from Miramax. Roger Avary, a fellow clerk at the store who would later share an Oscar with Tarantino for the screenplay to *Pulp Fiction*, described the place this way in the *New York Times Magazine*:

> Video Archives was less a video store than a film school. I mean, it has the best selection in Southern California. More importantly, they'd let us do what we want. We'd put a movie on—I mean, we didn't care if we offended anyone; Pasolini's *Salo* if need be, one of the vilest movies made—and we'd have these intense, eight-hour-long arguments about cinema. Customers would walk in and they'd get into it. It became this big clubhouse of filmmaking—and probably the best filmmaking experience anyone could ever get.

It made sense that *Vanity Fair* would refer to Tarantino's *Reservoir Dogs*, which came out in 1992, as "the first coffeehouse action movie," just as it made sense that Kurt Cobain would thank Tarantino in the liner notes to *In Utero*. As became clear from each and every magazine profile of Quentin Tarantino, the guy had developed an essential slacker trait: the encyclopedic brain. His compulsion to know things had turned his head into an immense Gen-X thrift shop—one filled with everything from *Coffy* to Cassavetes to Chow Yun-Fat. Even his West Hollywood apartment was curated. "He has filled it with his collections—movie posters, toys, comic books and '70s movie and television memorabilia, like board games of *Charlie's Angels, Starsky and Hutch*, and *Happy Days*," the *Times Magazine* noted.

The press, naturally, portrayed Tarantino as a Young Turk—a high school dropout turning Hollywood on its head—and he gamely played along. "You know, that is always the most exciting time in Hollywood, when they don't know what works anymore," he told *Newsweek* at the end of 1994, when *Pulp Fiction* had not only won the Palme d'Or in Cannes but had become an unlikely box-office behemoth. "First they'll hold on for as long as they can to these old dinosaurs. And then you have a *Pulp Fiction*, a film that doesn't play by the rules yet finds its audience." In spite of the bluster, Tarantino was a classicist at heart. He wrote his scripts in longhand: "You can't write poetry on a computer," he told *Vanity Fair*, a quote that makes me feel slightly less embarrassed about comparing Kurt Cobain's lyrics to John Donne. He refused to use a video monitor on set. He told people that he preferred to read books instead of screenplays, and, as *Newsweek* reported, "he announced to a table of critics at Cannes that if he ever gets a cellular phone they can write him off as a sellout."

Beck, like Tarantino, was a white boy who'd grown up in the ethnically diverse working-class neighborhoods of Los Angeles, and he, too, had managed to develop an encyclopedic brain in spite of a stunted SoCal education. In Beck's case it was musical data that was causing gridlock in his hippocampus. His records brimmed over with every musical genre imaginable: the blues, rap, country, punk, funk, folk, soul, bluegrass, techno, metal, free jazz, jangle pop, salsa, slow jams, spoken word, Southern-fried rock. Beck, too, was a classicist, a MoMA curator with two turntables and a microphone. The mass media wouldn't pick up on this at first—for a while, thanks to the lyrics of his 1994 hit "Loser," Beck would be written off as a sort of idiot-savant slacker sprite—but it didn't take long for people to realize that Beck's innocent-looking, tousle-haired noggin was in fact an organic, homegrown Music Genome Project.

If you look at them from another standpoint, there was yet another habit of mind that Beck and Quentin Tarantino had in common. Critics liked to gripe that the two of them didn't *believe* in anything, that Beck's records and Tarantino's movies amounted to dazzling virtuoso collages that had *nothing to say*, that both of them had at their core a kind of icy existential detachment. This was true. Not only was it true, it was, in the eyes of the Xers who bought the tickets, *one of the most attractive features of their work*, and the artists themselves didn't seem to disagree. "The Vietnam War and Watergate were a one-two punch that basically destroyed Americans' faith in their own country," Tarantino told *Premiere*'s Peter Biskind in 1994. "The attitude I grew up with was that everything you've heard is lies. The president is a monkey. I remember my parents saying, 'Fucked-up pigs, they're jerks.' " When *Pulp Fiction* won the Palme d'Or, Tarantino said he was surprised "because I don't make the kinds of movies that bring people together. I make the kinds of movies that split people apart."

Beck, in an unusually revealing 1997 interview with *Rolling Stone*, put it this way:

> I think my whole generation's mission is to kill the cliché.
> I don't know whether it's conscious all the time, but I
> think it's one of the reasons a lot of my generation are
> always on the fence about things. They're afraid to com
> mit to anything for fear of seeming like a cliché. They're
> afraid to commit to their *lives* because they see so much
> of the world as a cliché.

Maybe Partying Will Help: The Boomers Strike Back

Every idea is reducible to a cliché, and the function of a cliché is to castrate an idea.

—*Susan Sontag*

Hey, when are they gonna do the Altamont reunion?

—*John Popper of Blues Traveler, backstage at Woodstock '94*

By the time Kurt Cobain died, in April of 1994, I was on staff at *Entertainment Weekly*. The editors decided to put together a cover story, which meant that I was among the young reporters whose grim duty it was to call up people who'd had contact with Kurt and to ask them for their impressions. Somehow, in spite of my utter lack of street cred, I managed to get Steve Albini on the phone. The prospect of speaking with Steve Albini about Kurt Cobain's suicide unnerved me. The word on Albini, a member of eustachian-tube-shredding kamikaze-noise bands like Big Black and Rapeman, was that he could be ornery, cold, laceratingly precise—an ice pick of an interview. Bonehead questions would not be tolerated. Nirvana had recorded *In Utero* under Albini's gimlet-eyed watch, but he didn't like to be called a producer. He preferred the term *engineer*. If I used the wrong wording on the phone, I would be toast.

As it turned out, Albini behaved like a perfect gentleman. Not only was he polite, punctual, and open to a series of admittedly icky questions about a rock star who'd just relieved himself of his brains, but Albini happened to illuminate, as clearly as anyone could, the bizarre and paralyzing predicament in which Kurt Cobain had found himself. "No one else in the world has been in his situation," he told me on the phone. "That is, to go from being a carefree garage-rock gadfly to being on the vanguard of a very influential cultural and aesthetic change. And during the same period of time, he became a millionaire and a dope fiend and a father. I mean, he went through an enormous amount of experience in a very short period of time. That, combined with the sort of political and business nightmares that are associated with being in a large and important rock band, is the sort of pressure that you and I cannot fathom. I could never have endured what he had to endure. And the fact that he made it this long should probably be considered a testament to his sturdiness rather than the fact that he killed himself being an indicator of some weakness."

Within five years the world would once again be awash in pop stars who, like their boomer parents, craved nothing more than being as insanely famous as possible, but Cobain, much to the consternation of observers who seemed to think there was something un-American about wanting to be an artist instead of a celebrity, considered it loathsome to be rammed into the public eye. "He's not fundamentally a celebrity. He's not someone that craves attention. He's not someone that wanted to be doted over or pointed at. And he was put in the position of being all of those things," Albini told me. "Everyone in the world wanted to know what he was up to, what his wife was up to. His face was recognized. His behavior was scrutinized. It's the sort of thing that would make any sort of normal existence impossible. He couldn't go to a fuckin' movie. He couldn't go to a baseball game. He couldn't walk down the fuckin' street in his own neighborhood. How *on earth* could you prepare for that? How on earth could you accept that gracefully?"

With this in mind, maybe it's for the better that Cobain didn't stick around to see Woodstock '94.

Of course, nobody expected much from Woodstock '94, so it makes sense that nobody got much in return. Oh, maybe a squadron of fraternity brothers from Binghamton had fun sliding around in the mud, perhaps an extortionist pizza vendor made a killing, and presumably Sheryl Crow enjoyed a sweet spike in album sales after performing on the main stage. But as for sending renewed

Aquarian shock waves through the *Weltgeist*, Woodstock '94, also known as Wood$tock, also known as Woodschlock, also known as "No way, you *went* to that thing?!" was a bust.

Right from the start the enterprise was arranged behind a scrim of smug magnanimity: the guys who controlled the rights to the Woodstock brand, well, they were doing this for *you, maaaan*; they were mounting a sequel to the Great Mythical Hippie Sludge Convocation so that you, the follow-up generation, you sad, apathetic Xers, could sup from a ladle of their mind-expanding psychedelic stew. *It's not fair to hoard the magic! Pass it on, maaaan, pay it forward, slap on your boogie shoes and change the world, because the nineties are just the sixties turned upside down!* (Someone from the stage actually said that.) By putting together a sequel in which Joe Cocker and Trent Reznor would occupy the same bill, our boomer overseers were making the hopeful suggestion of a thread, a continuum from one generation to the next. Which was a laugh. Halfway through the festival, a barefoot Henry Rollins would treat himself to an anti-boomer dig. "Now they look like Don Henley and they're cashing in," he said. "Be sure to get your ya yas out before you go home, because they're getting the rest."

Le deuxième Woodstock had very little to do with the ethos of Gen X, but it had a lot to do with boomers reasserting their market dominance in a world that had replaced "I Want to Hold Your Hand" with "I want to fuck you like an animal." More than anything, the festival served as a three-day advertising campaign whose slogan might as well have been: *Boomers! We're Still Number One!*

Entertainment Weekly sent me up to Saugerties, New York, to cover the event. After five minutes anyone could tell that it was like a really big Springfield High School production of *Hair*—a Christo-scaled swath of performance art about "the sixties."

"This is Woodstock '94!" an announcer was saying from the stage. "We got TV this time!"

"Yeah, we got TV," a hippie muttered next to me. "We got a fuckin' mall."

That hippie spoke the truth. As I milled around for three days with yogurt-fragranced mud caking into Frankenstein boots around my ankles, I saw how an entire language of liberation and resistance had been watered down into meaningless commercial goop. The author and editor Thomas Frank has written extensively about the "commodification of dissent," and it's hard to think of it as anything more than an abstraction—or just a cool-sounding phrase—until you haul your ass to something like Woodstock '94 and see it with your own eyes. There on the crowded fields of Saugerties I saw a woman with a pot-leaf necklace and an Apple logo tattoo; I saw doves and peace symbols and tie-dyed tambourines and bongo drums; I saw the Greenpeace van and people dressed up as the Grateful Dead's dancing bears. I browsed through the Ohio Hempery and the Dharmaware booths. In the sky above hovered the Gulf Oil blimp. By 3:00 p.m. on the first day someone had already scrawled the word *Greedstock* on the water fountains.

There were corporate brands and there were ideological brands. "Peace & Love" was now a brand, which meant that it was hard to see "peace and love" as anything resembling a philosophy. To attend Woodstock '94 was to participate in the presumption that you were a Peace & Love consumer, an affiliation that had scant connection to your interest in the virtues of pax and Eros, but quite a lot to do with your interest in tossing around a Frisbee, donning garments made of hemp, burning incense, and garlanding your fire escape with wind chimes. The "meaning" of *peace* and *love* had long ago drained out of the words. The words were just felicitous sounds the tongue made, like *Nick at Nite* or Crate and Barrel.

It was amusing to listen to the patter constantly coming from the Woodstock '94 stage, because it didn't seem to have any connection to what was happening on the field. Sometimes, in between the bands, Wavy Gravy would come out—yes, Wavy Gravy, that dotty old boomer harlequin—and he would just . . . say stuff. The stuff sounded as though it had been scripted in advance by a team of Oscar Night comedy writers, and the idea behind it seemed to be: *Hey kids, crazy psychedelic high jinks are going down, and we're all cruising on the magic carpet now, and, holy guacamole, I think I see Timothy Leary gazing down at us from those thunderheads, and here we go—wheeeeeeeee!*

"The Felix the Cat Skeleton acid is shitty!" the emcee said. "Don't eat it! It will fuck you up!" Um, *really*? Was that a problem—were people truly wigging out on Felix the Cat Skeleton acid—or was that intended as a joke, *heh heh*? Nobody cared. It was just some guy onstage talking to himself.

"All I am saying is please move your tents"—delivered to the tune of John Lennon's "Give Peace a Chance," naturally.

"See, the human mind is kinda like a piñata. When it breaks open, there's a lot of surprises inside."

"The nineties are the sixties standing on your head." (Told you.)

"There's still a few things that the old guys can teach you." This gem delivered as Crosby, Stills & Nash were taking the stage. (*Yes, note to self: hire David Crosby as life coach.*)

I don't consider myself a Blues Traveler fan, but I have to hand it to John Popper, the leader of that band, for delivering a keen stab of commentary in the middle of their set. "The brown Pepsi that's been circulating is not that good," he said. "The Crystal Pepsi is okay."

At one point, the emcee looked out from the stage at the thousands of bodies pressed together and the tents sprouting like toadstools from the mud. "It feels like a community out there!" he informed us. Seconds after he said that, I watched a man wandering around looking for a place to rest his legs. "You mind if I sit right here?" he asked a group of revelers who'd managed to preserve the spotlessness of their Navajo blanket.

"Sorry," said one of the blanketeers. "That's saved."

X

It's comforting to think that that blanket lies slime-soaked and buried somewhere, probably in a landfill surrounded by pizza boxes and yards of Gore-Tex. Because once the rain started coming down on Woodstock '94, everybody sank into a pit of mud. Not *just* mud, either. Porta-potties tipped over. Food scraps and cigarette butts and condoms and lighter fluid got stirred into the broth. What people ended up slogging through, and swimming in, was a jambalaya of silt, feces, and debris. When I close my eyes, I can still summon forth the smell. It was sour and sweet, as pungent as old grapefruit, as persistent as spoiled milk left in an office fridge, canned-fishy, rotten-eggy, bacterial, cadaverous, ubiquitous. It climbed up the legs of my pants, crawled under my fingernails, and made a nest in my scalp. I still remember watching a river of zonked, sludge-splattered people moving slowly in circles, like Dante's masses being led through the gates of hell, while Joe Cocker belted out "Up Where We Belong."

Backstage, the singer from Blind Melon, Shannon Hoon, who would die of a cocaine overdose a few months later, floated around with an assistant. "All the questions I've been asked," he said, "and I haven't even been able to give the answer I want to give."

"NBC wants to do ten minutes," the assistant told him.

"I'm brain dead," Blind Melon Guy responded. "No."

Youssou N'Dour, the Senegalese singer known for ululating with Peter Gabriel, wandered into the frame. The assistant decided that it would be nice to have the two of them pose together for a picture. Hoon begged off—you could tell that he was in that romper room of the mind where every permutation of human contact was guaranteed to annoy him. The African troubadour took one look at him, his face beaming with kindly confusion, and said, "I don't know what you do. I don't know you. What do you do?"

Nothing and nobody had any significance, so it's logical that the only truly memorable incident that went down at Woodstock '94 was the one that seemed, at the time, to have no significance whatsoever. Green Day—a trio of bubblegum punks from the Bay Area who would, a decade later, emerge as a surprising symbol of political resistance with an album called *American Idiot*—hit the stage and got pelted with mud. Not just mud, but hundreds of hairy, stringy, aromatic clumps from the floating jambalaya. The crowd started tossing the clumps at the band, Billie Joe Armstrong couldn't resist throwing them back, and the notorious Green Day mud fight ensued, a melee that would end with bassist Mike Dirnt getting tackled by a security guard and chipping three of his teeth. "Hey, look at me," Armstrong said in the middle of the mud fight, taunting the crowd while feculent tumbleweeds dropped down on his head, "I'm a fuckin' idiot."

While he said that, I watched a couple of Woodstock II revelers picking up scoopfuls of mud and tucking them away in Tupperware containers. Ah, yes—a souvenir.

This Is Our Screen

> One day this conformist mob of mediocrity is on top. The next day you've got some aberrant genius kid like Spike Jonze who manages to pull something off.
>
> —*Film director Bennett Miller, in* Entertainment Weekly, *November 26, 1999*

"This film serves up the Sex Pistols," Darren Aronofsky is telling me. "We're making a punk movie and I want the audience in the movie theater to be a mosh pit of emotion and mayhem. When I grew up, I used to sneak into Manhattan late at night to go see *Eraserhead*, to go see *Stop Making Sense*, to go see *A Clockwork Orange*, because there were these underground, different, weird, freaky movies! *Requiem for a Dream* is hopefully part of that world. It's for people who have a hunger for something different."

It's May 20, 1999. Darren Aronofsky is on a lunch break while shooting his second film. He's wolfing down a plate of sturgeon at some alfresco Russian café in the Brighton Beach section of

Brooklyn. The sun is blindingly bright. The wind is gusting violently off the ocean. A waitress has taped a bouquet of artificial flowers to our table to keep them from blowing away. Aronofsky is excited. He talks fast. He eats fast.

He points to the east. "You see that white building? That's the start of my neighborhood. I was born and raised right down there. I almost burned down the boardwalk as a kid. I used to light fires under the boardwalk. Me and my friends were a bunch of arsonists." Graffiti taggers, too, supposedly. Even though Aronofsky graduated from Harvard, he likes to play up his juvenile delinquency. It's a bit of a Gen-X trademark, this Donny and Marie–style mix of the traditional and the transgressive. Herman Melville once said that a whaling ship had been his Harvard and his Yale. In Darren Aronofsky's case, his Harvard was Harvard, but his Yale was a skanky amusement park. He likes to say—in fact, says with the sort of regularity that suggests he's been practicing the line in front of a bathroom mirror since he was about nine years old— that he grew up in the shadow of Coney Island, and that the goal of his movies is to make you feel like you're taking your first nosedive on the Cyclone.

If we're talking about replicating the feeling of mosh pits and roller coasters, *Requiem for a Dream* would, when it came out a few months later, succeed. It would also be a tough film to watch, culminating in a long and frenzied montage of images of electroshock treatments, amputations, jailhouse abuse, and sexual degradation. But in 1999 "people who have a hunger for something different" were getting a chance to chow down. Wander into any random movie theater in that year and you might see cubicle drones sliding down a chute into John Malkovich's brain, frogs raining down on Los Angeles, or three terrified slackers getting lost in a forest haunted by an unseen sorceress.

Consider bullets. Strange things were happening with bullets in 1999. Nothing's more of a cliché in American movies than guys shooting guns, but 1999 was a year in which even the bullets learned how to bend the rules. Keanu Reeves dodged them like a kung fu phantom in *The Matrix*, Edward Norton shot one through his own face in *Fight Club* and kept on talking, and, in *Three Kings*, the audience straddled one as it ripped into a soldier's chest. Everywhere you looked in 1999, young movie directors and screenwriters were firing a big, swervy slug into the cinematic rule book. Spike Jonze, Charlie Kaufman, Kimberly Peirce, Sofia Coppola, Kevin Smith, David Fincher, David O. Russell, Wes Anderson, Alexander Payne, Richard Linklater, Paul Thomas Anderson—they'd been shaking things up for a decade, but 1999 felt like their annus mirabilis. Their weird-science visions didn't just dot the landscape. They dominated it.

These were filmmakers who had been weaned on *Cops* and Macintosh cut-and-pasting, on Public Enemy and Pac-Man, on endless reruns of *The Twilight Zone* and Blockbuster bong-load marathons of Altman and Truffaut. In the same way that there'd been a secret history of the eighties for college-radio rock snobs who preferred Hüsker Dü to Huey Lewis, and Big Daddy Kane to Billy Ocean, the stubbled cineasts of this new class were the kind of people who'd probably seen *Harold and Maude, Freaks*, and *The Killing of a Chinese Bookie* thirty times each. The more arcane, the better.

High and low, fast and slow, traditional and transgressive—their movies were all over the map, but what these auteurs had in common was a tacit contempt for the ten commandments of screenwriting. ("Thou shalt write a script with three distinct acts." "Thou shalt insert a plot point on page 27." "Thou shalt guarantee that the protagonist utters the words 'I'm getting too old for this shit' five seconds before he leaps out of a skyscraper to get away from the slo-mo fireball." "If the studio executive says, 'Change it,' thou shalt change it.") "The whole school of Act 1/Act 2/Act 3 is destructive to a thriving, growing cinema," Alexander Payne, the director of *Election*, told *EW*. "I think that for the last 20 years American films have lived under ideological restrictions which are as stringent as—if not more stringent than—the restrictions on

Eastern European films under Communism. You know, the hero has to triumph. The lovers have to reunite. The so-called liberal freethinkers running Hollywood are extremely conservative." The new X filmmakers were giving conventional Hollywood storytelling a wedgie. What that meant was that you could go to a theater in 1999 and wallow in the strange sensation of not being bored. You could watch a movie like *Magnolia* or *Being John Malkovich* or *The Blair Witch Project* or *Election* or *Boys Don't Cry* and have no idea what was going to happen next. This was refreshing. This was good. You were surprised. In fact, you were amazed that these movies ever got made. Could it be a mere coincidence, from the Gen-X standpoint, that an early X adopter like Michael Stipe had produced *Being John Malkovich*? "Hollywood narrative film is in its death throes right now," Stipe proclaimed in *EW*, "and people are looking for something else."

Darren Aronofsky insisted on doing everything his own way. For his first movie, a metaphysical thriller called π, he and his producers came up with a novel financing strategy: they asked every person they'd ever met for $100. Not only did the scheme raise $15,000, but as Aronofsky would later tell *EW*, it "probably helped our first-weekend box office numbers. It became a community of people connected with the film. There were a few hundred people out there going, 'Hey, I invested in this. Go see my movie. I'm a producer!' " With *Requiem for a Dream*, Aronofsky and his crew took care of all their editing and visual effects at Protozoa, their own private R&D facility in Greenwich Village. When it was done, *Requiem* would contain over two thousand separate cuts, and images in the film would riff on themselves in a kind of synaptic spray. Aronofsky began to refer to these sensory bombardments as "hip-hop montages." Jared Leto, one of the stars of *Requiem for a Dream*, compared the Protozoa method to something else: "It's like making crack out of cocaine," he said. Scenes between Leto and Jennifer Connelly, for instance, would be distilled—cut and cut and cut again, patiently boiled down to their adamantine essence.

"If you're growing up cutting and pasting constantly on your laptop or your home computer, yes, then you look at visual information and visual storytelling that way," Bill Block told *Entertainment Weekly* in 1999. Block was, at the time, the president of Artisan Entertainment, the independent film company that produced *Requiem for a Dream*. "You look at scenes as just chunks data chunks. To play with and move around. PlayStation Cinema, you could call it." You didn't merely "watch" a film; you mainlined a rush of visual and sonic data into your cranium.

Later I swing by Protozoa to see how the film is coming along, and Aronofsky ushers me into a rec room. He flicks a switch. Something descends from the ceiling. "This is our screen," he says. "We put the PlayStation away when we have journalists come over. But playing it on the big screen is really awesome."

X

The set of *Requiem for a Dream* was right across the street from a rest home for the elderly, which meant that old folks were constantly wandering over to see what was going on. One May afternoon a senior citizen with large, owlish glasses and a green wool cap worked his way up to one of the members of the film crew.

"What kind of picture will this be?" he asked.

"Sad," said the crew member. "It's a sad picture."

"Oh, I see," said the old man. "A sad picture. You know, a famous dramatist was born here. Right here! In Brighton Beach!"

"Neil Simon," said the crew member.

"That's the one!" said the old man.

It's safe to say that *Requiem for a Dream* may be the most un–Neil Simon movie ever made, and not just because of those hip-hop montages. The visual innovations that crept into Gen-X movies were cool, but what was really revolutionary was what the movies had to say. Just at the moment when alternative rock got tarted up and watered down in the middle of the nineties, movies stepped in to take up the slack: it was in films like *Being John Malkovich*, *Boys Don't Cry*, *Boogie Nights*, *Fight Club*, *Lost in Translation*, *Waking Life*, *Office Space*, and *The Matrix* that we got a sneaky critique of mass consumerism, celebrity worship, corporate drudgery, and other aspects of American culture that the boomers now seemed more than happy to wallow in.

All those films are strikingly different from each other, but if you rent a stack of DVDs and hold yourself a Gen-X film festival, it's illuminating to see what themes they have in common. In one movie after another, you encounter men and women trapped on a kind of psychic treadmill. This is literally true for Bill Murray in *Lost in Translation*: He's working out on an elliptical machine at the Park Hyatt Hotel in Tokyo, but he's not sure how to control it. The gears start grinding faster and faster. His legs whip back and forth. He can't stop, but he can't keep going. The only thing he can do to keep from having a heart attack is to leap off.

The characters in these movies suffer from varying degrees of stuckness. Usually they're so stuck that they don't even know they're stuck, and only drastic action will dislodge them from their trance. In *The Matrix*, Neo (the Keanu Reeves character) has to secure a pill from Morpheus (the Laurence Fishburne character) in order to see that he is actually a pruny embryonic slave floating around in a tank and being harvested for his energy. In *Being John Malkovich*, Cameron Diaz has to toboggan into Malkovich's head before she can realize that she's in love with Catherine Keener. Entire casts of Paul Thomas Anderson's films remain locked in the trance. Think of the porn stars strung out on blow, fame, and decay in *Boogie Nights*, or Tom Cruise as the delusional alpha-dog guru in *Magnolia*, or Adam Sandler all fogged up in a geek rage in *Punch-Drunk Love*. In the same way, *Requiem for a Dream*, based on a novel by Hubert Selby Jr., explores the lives of four people who've been snared into a hypnotic state of addiction. These movies are too oblique and complicated to promote anything as corny as a "message," but if they did, it would probably amount to two words: *wake up*. If the average Hollywood flick is made to reinforce the trance, the X movies endeavor to snap you out of it.

To take a more obscure example, let's consider *The Cruise*. *The Cruise* is a 1998 documentary directed by Bennett Miller, the obsessive craftsman who later helped Philip Seymour Hoffman win an Oscar with *Capote*. *The Cruise* is also a tone poem about solitude, which is only fitting, because the entire crew on the movie consisted of Bennett Miller—writer, director, soundman, camera operator, gaffer, and grip. Thanks to digital video, the collaborative art of moviemaking has been opened up to agoraphobics with iMacs. "I have either a neurological or pathological disorder that prohibits me from collaborating with people," Miller told *Entertainment Weekly*. "This technology was made for me. At my own pace, according to my own whims and instincts, I could pick up a camera and shoot without even speaking to anybody."

Although the guerrilla technology of *The Cruise* made it feel ahead of the curve—it was one of the first films released in theaters to be shot entirely with a handheld, and this was years before the arrival of YouTube and TMZ—the movie is really more of a wistful look back. Seen now, *The Cruise* is about something that seemed to be evaporating from the American atmosphere at the tail end of the twentieth century. The entire film is about a young Xer named Timothy "Speed" Levitch. Speed lives in New York and makes a living, sort of, by emceeing bus tours of Manhattan. But calling him a mere "tour guide" is like calling Hunter S. Thompson a Beltway pundit. Whatever remains of New York City's bohemian spirit is embodied in this charming, exasperating, sometimes profound, sometimes profoundly full-of-shit oracle of liberation. Homeless, prone to wearing purple velvet blazers and *Alice in*

Wonderland top hats, and endowed with a high, squeaky voice that calls to mind Bugs Bunny doing a public recitation of Carlos Castaneda, Speed wanders around the city all day and crashes on couches at night. He's the last man slacking—his way of life runs aggressively against the grain of the dot-com boomtown zeitgeist of the late 1990s. Everywhere you look, Gen Xers are starting to get gravity-defyingly rich—in New York and San Francisco, in Seattle and Austin—and yet here on the screen Speed Levitch keeps jabbering away ("The anticruise is an attempt to imprison us!"), elbowing us in the ribs, winking, alluding to something we seem to have forgotten or misplaced, something we need to wake up to again. What is it? Consider the penultimate scene in the film: Speed Levitch stands with his arms outstretched at the foot of the twin towers of the World Trade Center. He begins to spin around and around like a kid trying to make himself dizzy. Finally, having achieved playground vertigo, he lies down on the ground and casts his eyes upward at the towers. "I am cruising" he says a few beats later. "I am cruising because I have dedicated myself to all that is creative and destructive in my life right now, and I am equally in love with every aspect of my life right now, and all the ingredients that have caused me turmoil, and all the ingredients that have caused me glory. I am the living whispered warning in the Roman general's ear: 'Glory is fleeting.' And in that verb, that active verb, *fleeting*—there I live; there I reside, at this moment. I've dedicated myself to the idiom *I don't know.*"

X

That same afternoon on the set in Brooklyn, a kid navigated his way to Aronofsky's side and started peppering him with questions. He was about ten years old, and he'd been watching the action from the street, but apparently standing on the sidelines was not going to suffice.

"Can I have some headphones?" the kid said.

"Give him some," Aronofsky said to a crew member.

The kid said he'd heard the movie cost $4 million. "That's just my fee," Aronofsky said. "That's what I get." (He was joking. The budget for the entire movie was not much bigger than $4 million, and Aronofsky's own cut was likely to be minuscule.)

"I wanna be an actor," the kid said.

"Eh, don't be an actor," said Aronofsky. "They're all messed up."

"So," the kid said, "you spend four million dollars on it, you get eight million dollars back?"

"How *old* are you?" Aronofsky said.

The kid's grandmother, a classic Russian babushka, yelled at the kid and tugged at him to leave. "Five minutes!" the kid snapped back. He was wearing baggy jailhouse jeans and a Nautica baseball cap. He studied the video monitor for a while, and then, sneakily, when Aronofsky was looking the other way, he managed to slide his ass into the director's chair. "Action!" he barked.

Aronofsky looked around and rolled his eyes. "Little Steven Spielberg here," he murmured. "The kid's taking over."

Hot Freaks: Prague 1991

> A little nation, by their own estimate, of scant consequence in the councils of the great.
>
> —*Derek Sayer, writing about the Czech people in* The Coasts of Bohemia: A Czech History

The kids in Prague had their own "Smells Like Teen Spirit," and the great thing about their anthem of choice was that it was incorrigibly cheesy. Everywhere you went in Eastern Europe in the spring of 1991, you heard "Wind of Change" by the Scorpions. The Czechs saw nothing ironic about this. They didn't say, "We are the generation that has overthrown tyranny, we can speak freely for the first time since the Prague Spring of 1968, and we have chosen to memorialize the success of our revolution by rocking out to cheesy Teutonic hair metal—*heh heh heh.*"

No, "Wind of Change" meant something to them. I remember hanging out in a disco somewhere outside of Karlovy Vary when the DJ played "Wind of Change," and as soon as the kids on the dance floor heard Klaus Meine's mournful, hamboney whistling, they stood at attention as if it were the national anthem. There are Americans who were in Prague during that period who still, to this day, get choked up when they hear "Wind of Change" on the radio, which must be incredibly confusing to their friends.

The reflexive media line on Prague was that Gen Xers had poured into the city because the beer was excellent and cheap, but you could say the same thing about Milwaukee. Milwaukee didn't have a revolution. A revolution—a real one, a genuine wind of change—swept across Eastern Europe in the late eighties and early nineties, and for some of us it would be the only chance to see anything like it. If you stayed in Prague long enough to sponge up a sudsy pool of "the Czech spirit," you came to realize that it was a curious echo of the way that we, as Xers, wanted to see ourselves. The Czechs had a term, *malost*, for the "littleness" that was their psychic and geographical fate. (Coincidentally, in *Generation X*, Douglas Coupland uses a similar term, *lessness*, which he defines as a "philosophy whereby one reconciles oneself with diminishing expectations of material wealth. *'I've given up wanting to make a killing or be a bigshot. I just want to find happiness and maybe open up a little roadside café in Idaho.'* ") The Czechs had serious matters to contend with, of course, but the way they did so was valiantly charming. They were better at this *malost* stuff than we were. In fact, the students who had risen up during the strikes and demonstrations of the Velvet Revolution were doing something that many of us had presumed to be impossible: they were saving the world, or least saving their humble portion of it. Having been sandwiched for centuries between European superpowers, the Czech people had learned how to fight oppression with *style*, with a smirk, with a dashing kind of strategic disengagement. Their national epic, Jaroslav Hašek's novel *The Good Soldier Švejk*, concerns a Czech soldier in the bureaucratic Austro-Hungarian army who never quite makes it to the battlefield, although he does spend plenty of time drinking, chatting, and getting caught up in one slapstick-absurdist caper after another. Is Švejk a moron or is he a crafty avant-garde loafer—the dissident as performance artist? No one can really tell, and that's the point. "The best thing you can do now," Švejk tells a character at one point in the story, "is to pretend to be an idiot."

Over many years the Czechs had figured out how to outsmart their overlords without always looking smart and how to stand up for their principles without necessarily standing out. In the eyes of a young American in 1991, such an approach came across as unimpeachably cool. (It's also worth pointing out that Jaroslav Hašek died before finishing *The Good Soldier Švejk*, and an unfinished national epic has to qualify as a slacker milestone.) The Czech spirit was in bloom in 1991. You saw punk rock defiance and absurdist gags everywhere you looked. Prague had delivered a Cooler King moment on the geopolitical stage: having liberated their country in 1989, the Czechs had picked Václav Havel to lead it. Václav Havel, an experimental playwright, an underground rock connoisseur, and a founding member of the Charter 77 dissident movement, who'd spent years wasting away in Communist prisons, was now one of the most influential diplomats in Europe. During his first few weeks in office after becoming the president of Czechoslovakia, Havel made a point of setting up a one-on-one meeting with the lord of the American underground, Lou Reed. The motorcycle-over-the-barbed-wire implausibility of that! Well, it became contagious. For a while the streets of Prague buzzed with a Banksy-like penchant for pranking. After the triumph of the

Velvet Revolution, a twenty-three-year-old Czech artist named David Černý climbed atop on old Soviet tank that was mounted on a pedestal and painted it hot pink.

What Xer could resist? Going to Prague meant that you weren't willing to settle for bohemia—you were upgrading to Bohemia itself, a place where the president of the country shook the walls of the castle with "Sister Ray."

When I was briefly in Prague, I got the impression that more than a handful of our fellow expatriates had first been exposed to the struggles of the Czech people by reading *The Unbearable Lightness of Being*—or maybe by seeing the movie version, which starred a destabilizingly sexy Lena Olin in a bowler hat. *The Unbearable Lightness of Being* is almost a required text for anyone who wants to get a handle on the X sensibility. Toward the end of Milan Kundera's novel, he carries the reader along on a mesmerizing digression. You'll find it in the section called "The Grand March."

There, Kundera brilliantly explores the concept of kitsch. Kitsch, he writes, is a denial of reality. More to the point, it is a denial of *shit*. Kitsch is that form of sentimental propaganda in which the fecal truths of human existence are erased from a snapshot, excised from a speech, and bleeped out of a song. "And no one knows this better than politicians," Kundera writes. "Kitsch is the aesthetic ideal of all politicians and all political parties and movements. Those of us who live in a society where various political tendencies exist side by side and competing influences cancel or limit one another can manage more or less to escape the kitsch inquisition: the individual can preserve his individuality; the artist can create unusual works. But whenever a single political movement corners power, we find ourselves in the realm of *totalitarian kitsch*."

Kitsch, as laid out by Kundera, might just be the thing that unites Xers in scorn. Xers bristle when they're told how to vote, how to behave, what to listen to, how to squander their time. They recoil at any hint of a presumption that *this is how things are done* or, even worse, *this is what you're supposed to think.* I suspect this intellectual reflex has a lot to do with why Xers are reluctant to fall in line behind any kind of preordained political agenda—whether it's coming from the Democrats or the Republicans or a movement further out on the fringe—and it's probably a healthy, sensible response to the cultural and philosophical dominance of the boomers. By the middle of the seventies, boomer kitsch was already carved in granite. If you listened to classic rock radio stations when they celebrated some churchy three-day weekend devoted to the best songs of all time, the songs never varied, and they were hammered into your brain like a catechism: "Stairway to Heaven," "Free Bird," "A Day in the Life," "You Can't Always Get What You Want," "Imagine." If you followed politics, you were told that American political philosophy *always* boiled down to an incredibly boring and ludicrous binary: conservative versus liberal. If you watched television, you absorbed an endlessly flickering stream of historical footage—Nixon sweating through a televised debate, the march on Washington, the Kennedy motorcade in Dallas, stoned and frolicking flower children in Golden Gate Park, teargassed frenzies in Chicago in '68, apostolic skinny-dippers at Woodstock—which sanctified the sixties in a way that placed these events somehow beyond inquiry or inspection. *Here is history, my child—open your mouth and place it on your tongue.* It is not that the events themselves were fraudulent when they happened—the march on Washington remains a pivotal and inspiring flash point in American history. The point is that repetition is stultifying. Glaze these events over with too many layers of nostalgic, Forrest Gumpian gloss and the spirit that mobilized them in the first place fades away. Turn change into kitsch and you've inspired no one to change anything. You've told them that change has already happened—*it was beautiful, maaaan, you should've been there*—and you've frozen the very concept of transformation in a glob of museum-ready amber. "When I say 'totalitarian,'" Kundera writes, "what I mean is that everything that infringes on kitsch must be banished for life: every display of individualism (because a deviation from the collective is a spit in the eye of the smiling brotherhood); every doubt (because anyone who starts doubting details will end by doubting life itself); all irony (because in the realm of kitsch everything must be taken quite seriously). . . ."

The sudden presence of American Xers in Prague after the strikes and demonstrations of the Velvet Revolution had something to do with this—with our desire to see change happening in real time before it was sanctified, unspooled in slo-mo, and tastefully paired with a soundtrack for a PBS special. Maybe something told us that a city full of pink tanks and presidential summits with Lou Reed would thrive, at least for a while, as a nesting place for a sensibility that was profoundly and pugnaciously pro-individual.

X

One night in Prague, seduced by the prospect of homemade fruit dumplings, I traveled out to the suburbs to visit the home of Jiří and Jana Tůma. Jiři was a department chair at a Czech technical university. The students there called him "the old Communist." His wife, Jana, was a doctor, and the Eastern-bloc Mayberry kitsch of their domestic life suggested that they might have a lot in common with any random couple of respectable, middle-class Methodists from Topeka. They had a new TV, a remodeled kitchen, a collection of trinkets that they'd accumulated while visiting Cuba.

The Tůmas had not been dissidents in the Communist years. They'd backed the wrong horse. While outcasts like Havel were languishing in prison, the Tumas were sunbathing in Havana. They'd traveled abroad. They'd pursued their professional ambitions. Silent complicity with the Communist regime had enabled them to enjoy, at least up until the Velvet Revolution, a life of worry-free comfort.

Mrs. Tůma served the apricot dumplings after dinner, and they were massive. They were like sponges. Lukewarm and doughy, smeared with butter and sugar and farmer's cheese, the dumplings began, almost from the moment they entered your esophagus, to suck up every ounce of liquid in your body and dehydrate your brain. As I tried to eat them, Mrs. Tůma decided to tell me the story about the kittens.

The Tůmas had a cat. While we sat at the table bloating ourselves on apricot dumplings, the cat batted away at a couple of Fidel Castro bobbleheads on a bookshelf. Mrs. Tůma told me that the cat had given birth to five kittens a few months ago, but they had decided they didn't want them. Mrs. Tůma groped around for a word in English to describe what had befallen the kittens. "Et . . . ta . . . etta . . . etha . . ." She went to the shelf to get an old, worn Czech-English dictionary. She flipped through it and found the word. "Ether!" she said. "Ether!" She smiled a warm apricot-dumpling smile. "We put da kittens in a box and close it up and put in da ether and kill dem."

That dinner with the Tůmas made a big impression on me, and the next morning, puffed up with the sort of naïve outrage that recent college graduates are so skilled at, I wrote the following words in my journal—a journal that I plan to burn as soon as I am finished with this book:

"I couldn't help thinking that Mr. Tůma was some kind of a sellout, more than willing to bend over and pull the proper knobs in order to get his cozy little life in the suburbs. (Ironic that the 'best' Communists lived in plush surroundings, like the most bourgeois members of America's middle class; I thought Communists were supposed to be good, simple, stark-living workers. Ha!)

"What kind of man puts comfort above principle?"

Ha.

Gold Soundz

> Everyone I know knows somebody, or knows somebody who knows somebody, who's made $10 million before the age of 35.
>
> —*Nina Munk, in* Fortune, *March 16, 1998*

> Well, I can't forget the sound, 'cause it's here to stay
> The sound of people chasing money and money getting away
>
> —*Uncle Tupelo, "Whiskey Bottle"*

> What's risotto?
>
> —*Netscape's chief technology officer, Marc Andreessen, quoted in the* Los Angeles Times, *October 28, 1996*

One day everyone woke up and discovered money. At least that's how it felt. Those college friends of yours who were bound for Wall Street and Madison Avenue and Sand Hill Road—okay, yes, they'd always been up front about money. They wanted it. They wanted a lot of it. They were perfectly blunt about that, and not even the stock market crash of 1987 could deter them from pursuing it in extremis. But for several years in the nineties you could still stumble upon islands of Gen-X creatives who tended to keep the concept of filthy lucre at arm's length. If you brought up the topic with that nobly unconventional friend of yours who was teaching English in Bangkok or writing a novel in Belfast or working as a line cook in Berkeley, he or she would take a sort of scoffing pride in having no idea what you were talking about. About money it was chic to be clueless. Then all of a sudden it was not.

A memo went out. A microchip started bleating out instructions behind your ear. Overnight, the line cook changed her mind and decided to get an MBA. The English teacher launched a hedge fund. The novelist brainstormed a business plan for a new Web site and flew west to drum up some venture capital. You found yourself for the first time tapping strange little acronyms into your computer: AMZN, HPQ, PFE, WMT, INTC, MSFT, CSCO, ORCL. You wanted to see how your new friends were doing. Your new friends were the stocks that you were slowly and miraculously amassing in your 401(k).

Your friends were doing very well. Corporations were engineered to exploit and enslave you, sure, of course, but wait—this 401(k) was a magical thing! If you worked at a company that had one, the company pinched off a morsel of every paycheck and stashed it away in a fund somewhere. If yours was a really nice company, they would *match* each of those morsels—they'd just give it to you, free. The idea was that your little fund would grow and grow and, voilà, one day you'd have something to retire on. You would not have to subsist on Alpo and Bud Light, and, anyway, with the stock market swelling like Violet Beauregarde on blueberry gum, it seemed sort of silly to worry about that, because everyone was getting rich. Not rich in the robber baron sense—although that was starting to happen, too—but rich enough to make you want to stick with your job. Rich enough to make you see why a promotion could lead to some lovely ancillary benefits. Rich enough to allow you to consume sushi so delicious that it made your eyes roll back. Rich enough to help you forget all about those humiliating job interviews back in 1991. Sometimes the best way to make people care about money is to give them some.

X

How did this happen? Well, if you had resigned yourself to a lifetime of honorable squalor, if you had internalized the notion that your impractical and arcane Gen-X obsessions would never make money, and if you liked to cheer yourself up with the idea that rich people only became rich because they were all too willing to endure a lifetime of soul-deadening and ass-flattening office misery, then maybe it was the cover of *Time* magazine on February 19, 2006, that smacked you on the ears. If you passed it in an airport, you felt a spritz of sweat on your brow. Maybe a little geyser of burrito acid-refluxed in your sternum.

There was Marc Andreessen, twenty-four years old, barefoot, sitting on a gilded throne with a look of royal boredom on his face. Here is what it said on the cover of the magazine: "The Golden Geeks. They invent. They start companies. And the stock market has made them instantaires." Here is what it said inside the magazine: Andreessen, as part of the team that had launched the Netscape Internet browser, was now worth something in the neighborhood of $58 million. On August 9, 1995, Netscape had rolled the dice with an IPO. An IPO—you were starting to learn this stuff now, it was becoming part of your vocabulary—was an initial public offering. With the stock market soaring, a private company could raise mountains of cash by going public, by whipping up a frenzy of hype for the company and then selecting a day on which to sell shares in it. If someone like Marc Andreessen already owned a stash of those shares because he'd been lucky or smart enough to, in the chummy parlance of the boardroom, get in on the ground floor, then for him an IPO operated like the matter transporter in *Star Trek*: he would be beamed, in the blink of an eye, from a messy cubicle crop-dusted with Doritos crumbs to the verdant and gleaming fields of planet Cash. He would be exactly the same person, except that he would be infinitely richer. He would still go to work in a place that was like a stoner's beanbaggy crash pad. You could see that guy right now, sailing along on a magenta Razor scooter down the halls of a sunny, exposed-pipe Palo Alto warehouse, carrying a ferret under his arm for Bring a Rodent to Work Day, flying in the Roots for a random Friday office party, strafing the cubicles with toilet paper on Act Like an Adolescent Day, blowing off steam for an hour or two at the foosball table . . . with President Clinton . . .

The impact of this phenomenon on Generation X was seismic. If a scientist had wanted to introduce avarice into the X bloodstream, he couldn't have come up with a better mode of mass infection than the dot-com boom. The dot-com boom spoke to us. It mesmerized us, it flattered us, it whispered in our ears about *paradigm shifts* and *monetized eyeballs* and *hierarchy-free, pet-friendly office spaces*. In a delicate way it preyed on everything the Xer believed in. The dot-com boom reached out a gloved hand and said: *Luke, I am your father.*

That's because the people building these new companies were *not* corporate tools—not yet, at least. They were DIY computer-lab oddballs and visionaries! They were passionate! Independent! Visibly out of shape! Totally wary of mainstream media attention! They wore Sebadoh T-shirts and got lunch from taco trucks. They were Trekkies with taste. They were creating—from scratch—new routes with which to navigate the world, and they were overthrowing all the old ways of watching and selling and sharing things. "The PC revolution happened in the 1980s," proclaimed Halsey Minor, the thirty-one-year-old chairman of CNET: The Computer Network, which was pioneering the whole idea of making television and online services intersect. "It destroyed the hegemony of companies like IBM. The media revolution is going to destroy media companies."

Yes! Kill your idols!

For a while it looked as though the revolution might even destroy companies themselves—at least companies that insisted on clinging to antediluvian stuff like dress codes and executive suites. Now, culture-jamming ideas were being hatched over PlayStation sessions, Econ 101 was merging with chaos theory, and your colleagues were printing out business cards with job titles such as guru of fun, minister of propaganda, and chief imagination officer. As *BusinessWeek* later put it:

> Just as the French tried briefly to substitute the label "citizen" for the more bourgeois "Monsieur" and "Madame" as part of their revolution, militant dot-commers

adopted titles that reflected their Brave New World. "It was a matter of doing away with everything that seemed to reek of the old," says Donna Hoffman, a professor of management at Vanderbilt University's Owen School of Management, who specializes in e-commerce. "The feeling was, 'We're not like dad. We're different. The Internet calls for a different response. We're going to make new rules. We need new titles.' "

As for Andreessen, here was a generational comrade who had managed to make himself gaspingly rich, and yet had done so without turning into some *American Psycho* clone. Andreessen was, in his apple-cheeked, Illinois-science-fair way, every bit as eccentric and contrarian as you wanted to be, and now he had in his possession enough money to change the world. These dot-com pioneers wanted America to suck less, and they were amassing enough capital to make it happen. "But money isn't all that's at stake: They're also jockeying for a place in the history of the information revolution," wrote Amy Harmon in the *Los Angeles Times* in the fall of 1996.

For amid their rigorously pragmatic approach to the world lurks an incongruous and often facile devotion to the social promise of high technology. . . . They are marked by the acutely self-conscious irony of their generation, half-believing skeptics' contention that their success resulted from being in the right place at the right time, rather than any true innovation. But this new generation of entrepreneurs shares with past generations an intensity of dedication to their work. And in many ways they are savvier, striving as they are to combine technology with communication and media. Smart, irreverent, somewhat cocky and definitely scared, they are growing up fast, learning to handle their fame and fortune and trying to balance personal relationships with business. . . .

Jerry Yang and Dave Filo, according to the *Los Angeles Times*, had cooked up Yahoo! "in a cramped trailer at Stanford." Like a couple of Dungeons & Dragons droolers mapping out their vast imaginary landscapes, they wanted to keep track of all the cool sites they stumbled across on the World Wide Web, so they began to put together a list. The list got bigger. The list became a database. The database began to lure millions of users. Sequoia Capital decided to chip in a million bucks. Within a year, Yang and Filo were heading for an IPO. After the IPO, Filo was worth tens of millions of dollars, but he still slept underneath his desk now and then, and he still puttered around the Bay Area in a 1980 Datsun that was prone to stalling. Even more Xishly, he seemed to have a sixth sense that something was bound to go wrong, not with Yahoo!, per se, but with all the hot air that was puffing up the dot-com bubble into a Wall Street whoopee cushion. "The pressure is a little worse now because we're a public company," he told Harmon. "The big funds and institutions are one thing, but when the little people buy stock in you and the stock goes down and they lose their money, that's kind of a bummer."

X

The dot-com boom had one potent ingredient whose talismanic allure cannot be understated. It had California. Although tech mania was breaking out all over the place—in Seattle, in Austin, in New York City—Silicon Valley and San Francisco remained the indisputable vortices of the revolution. And California—well, who can resist it? California is the myth that keeps on mything. Everybody knew that the Bay Area had been the Xanadu of the sixties, the breeding ground for Mario Savio and the Free Speech movement, for psychedelia, for the Summer of Love. If the Pacific Coast was once again sending out shock waves, didn't you want to be a part of that? To go west *where it's all happening, man*—wasn't that a rite of passage in America?

I remember traveling from New York to San Francisco for a few days during the very crest of the dot-com delirium. It was the middle of winter, and the sun—that California sun that you want to bask in for hours, the sun that seems to loosen your limbs and massage your scalp with olive oil—was basting itself all over the buildings of South Park. South Park, an emerald affixed to the ring of San Francisco's South of Market district, was the very nucleus of new media, the home of everything from *Wired* to Napster. There was an oval park in the middle of it, and start-ups ringed around the park like knights at the round table. Almost as an ironic emoticon wink to the Haight-Ashbury era, some of the building facades had been painted shades of Day-Glo purple and green. I could hear the drone of saws and sandblasters and cement mixers—an aria of gold-rush construction. I bought a macchiato at Caffe Centro and found a park bench under the trees. I watched a couple of coltish women my age dangling on swings in the sunshine, kicking their tanned legs, laughing, dreaming of all the money they would one day roll in—they didn't have flowers in their hair, but they had sprigs of green. "Bliss was it in that dawn to be alive / But to be young was very heaven!" Totally. The Netscape IPO had happened right around the time that Jerry Garcia had died, and there was a joke going around the Bay Area that, according to *Newsweek*, perfectly nailed the way a new San Francisco sensibility had elbowed out an old one:

> **Q:** What's the last thing Jerry Garcia said before he had his heart attack?
>
> **A:** "Netscape opened at *what?*"

The boom made it impossible for you to pretend that you didn't care about money. Even if you didn't quit your horse-and-buggy, eastern seaboard job in order to join the wired robber barons of the West—and plenty of people did—you could feel the ripple effect of the boom every time you sat down at your desk and logged on to your computer. There, if you happened to own a few trial-balloon shares of Cisco or Intel or Amazon.com, you could see that tiny stock market ticker right on your home page, and before long it became a daily habit—maybe even an hourly one, if you were really obsessive-compulsive—to type in a few letters, make note of the rising price of those shares, and wallow in the warm, bathlike realization that you'd just made *money*. Holy shit.

Maybe you'd never even considered the possibility before. As a Gen Xer you more or less *expected* to get reamed, so maybe you figured that you, in your golden years, would wind up like a geriatric version of those clods in *Clerks*, muttering vulgarities and schlepping your way through the service sector until the grim reaper showed up at the video shop to rent *Scarface*. But what if? What if you *could* retire? What if you could retire at, say, forty? What if you could retire at forty with, like, Marc Andreessen money? What if you could achieve . . . The Sum? The Sum meaning: enough money to do whatever you wanted without ever having to work. *The Sum*—it was painful to imagine it. The Sum was a lot of rare Kiwi pop singles on vinyl, and it was a video library with every grindhouse movie ever made, and it was back issues of every single issue of *Sassy*. But why think small? You could buy *Sassy*. You could relaunch it. You could make indie films. You could become a *patron*—a modern-day Medici, anonymously, wantonly spreading your abundance around like dandelion seeds. The Sum meant all the time in the world to slack. It meant trips to Thailand and Nepal, Morocco and Lapland, Patagonia and Tenerife. But The Sum did not speak merely of luxury and idleness. No, it could be highminded. The Sum had a soul! Just think of the literacy programs you could launch, the bolstering of environmental land trusts, the organic soup kitchens, the Babylonian gardens and Athenian libraries for homeless people. With The Sum you could *do something*.

X

Anyway, a lot of people had the same idea, and a lot of them couldn't tell a line of computer code from a snippet of ancient Sumerian.

What turned a boom into a bust was the stock market crash in the spring of 2000, yes, but what signaled the waning of Silicon Valley's significance as a haven for enterprising freaks was the invasion of MBAs in the late 1990s. "There was some-thing oddly charming about the geeks who made up the first wave of Internet entrepreneurs," *Time* magazine wistfully mused in September 1999.

> Social misfits pounding out code in their computer-science labs—these people deserved professional success. But after the Wright Brothers, you get Frank Lorenzo. And so this summer Silicon Valley was flooded by the Second Wave: fast-talking business-school grads whose interest in technology is limited to how it will make them money. This is Silicon Valley in the IPO age. Geeks are history; they're all capitalists now.

The tech world had always seen plenty of crackpot schemes, but now they were legion. Now we entered the age of Kozmo.com and Furniture.com—the first of which thought it made business sense to let you order a roll of Lifesavers online and have them delivered to your door with the help of a sleek $250 million messenger service; the second of which figured you'd be keen to stock up on expensive beds and sofas that you'd never had the chance to bounce around on. This was the age of Zap.com, Zelerate.com, and Zoza.com, of eLetter.com, eTown.com, eCircles.com, and ePod.com, of Pets.com, Petstore.com, PetSmart.com, and Petopia.com. Now, merely to see their domain names is to marvel at the absurdity.

Yes, in case you're repressing the memory, this was such a bizarre moment in American capitalism that companies were actually hissing and baring fangs at each other in a battle to sell kitty litter over the Web. Someday, apparently, Web sites would change the very essence of domestic pet care. "I'm out of dog food and my cat's box needs new litter," wrote Philip J. Kaplan, the chief mortician at the brilliant FuckedCompany Web site, which delighted in the demise of one boneheaded idea after another. "I know what I'll do: I'll order Dog Chow and Fresh Step online from a sock puppet and then I'll watch the dog starve and the cat shit all over the house while I wait for it to be delivered!"

By 1999 the people who showed up in *Fortune* stories about Silicon Valley were not lovable first-wave misfits with adult acne and Asperger's syndrome. They were a whole new group of glad-handing interlopers from the land of Khaki. They came with their Harvard MBAs, with their fondness for win-win situations and first-mover advantages and stealth mode and opening the kimono. They had spreadsheets that could show you, beyond a shadow of a doubt, why there was an untapped online market of approximately $3 billion for toilet paper. "Unlike their predecessors, Silicon Valley's new entrepreneurs don't spend their time talking about operating systems or Java applications or HTML code," wrote Romesh Ratnesar and Joel Stein in *Time* in the fall of 1999. "They talk about capturing eyeballs, forging strategic partnerships and 'making the dogs eat the dog food.' In the '80s they would have been financing junk-bond takeovers. Today these lapsed consultants and investment bankers are fleeing six-figure job offers from Wall Street for the opportunity to build their own empires." A few days earlier, in August of 1999, the cover of *Fortune* bore the headline .COM FEVER and showed a dashing Harvard MBA named Josh Keller carrying a backpack and walking along some train tracks in a classic enshrinement of the "go west, young man" myth. "Harvard MBA Josh Keller turned down a lucrative job at Campbell Soup," the cover said. "He's taking $50,000 a year to join a Web startup." "God, to not do the Internet now would be such a huge mistake," Keller explained from a pay phone in Kentucky as he made his way across the country to some sunshiny start-up utopia. "This is not filling in the bubbles. It is not multiple choice. This is creating something from scratch."

It's fascinating to go back and look at this dot-com coverage now, because everything that people were saying makes perfect sense, and yet now we know that they were all careening toward a very steep cliff. The *Fortune* cover story, written by Betsy Morris, opened with a snapshot of Patrick Mullane, a thirty-one-year-old husband and father who was in the process of turning down a fine opportunity as a consultant—a salary in the six figures, a $30,000 signing bonus, and a chance to wipe the slate clean of all those tuition debts after leaving Harvard Business School—in order to be, instead, part of the start-up pandemonium. "Everything around me was shifting," Mullane told the magazine.

> All his courses seemed linked to the revolutionary changes ushered in by the Internet. Entrepreneurs and recent B-school graduates paraded through, electrifying students with speeches about their companies. Michael Dell packed the room.... Thirty years from now, when your grandson asks where you were for the Big One, you won't have to say, Well, I was shoveling shit in Louisiana. "That's how I felt," said Mullane. "I didn't want to miss the Big One. I didn't want to miss the next Industrial Revolution. I didn't want to have any regrets."

Who were these folks? Well, said *Fortune*, "They're risk takers, mercenaries. They have—get this!—an in-your-face attitude about business. They don't wear wingtips. And the last thing they want to do is conform." And, "To be fair, this new breed of MBA is genuinely enchanted with all things nimble and entrepreneurial, and profoundly disenchanted with lumbering, process-oriented corporate America." And, "Failure is a plus in the Internet Age: It's called experience."

A lifetime's worth of experience was right around the bend.

In 2000 the stock market crashed. Funding shriveled up. Thousands of dot-coms went under, and thousands of Xers hitched a ride back to reality. Now Xers cared about money, and now, once again, they had a lot less of it. Pretty soon we had a new recession, a new

President Bush, a new war in Iraq—it was 1991 all over again. In February 2002, exactly two years after my glimpse of that sun-dappled Gen-X wonderland in San Francisco, the dot-com implosion had so gutted the South Park neighborhood that junkies and drifters were starting to reclaim it. One day, as recalled later in the *San Francisco Chronicle*, a performance artist drove a truck into this high-tech ghost town, dumped a pile of tumbleweeds in the middle of the park, and let the California breeze carry them across the grass.

Lost in Translation

> One should, for example, be able to see that things are hopeless and yet be determined to make them otherwise. This philosophy fitted on to my early adult life, when I saw the improbable, the implausible, often the "impossible" come true.
>
> —*F. Scott Fitzgerald, in his 1936 essay "The Crack-Up"*

Among the movies that came out in 1999, right in the middle of the most oily and feverish phase of the dot-com boom, two stand out: *Fight Club* and *Being John Malkovich*. Those two films capture something of that moment, and they give full expression to the idea that Generation X was shaking its way through some changes.

At the beginning of *Fight Club*, Edward Norton's character is an insomniac drone. He comes home from his corporate job, sits on the john, and opens a catalog to coo masturbatorially over dust ruffles and coffee tables. "Like so many others, I had become a slave to the IKEA nesting instinct," Norton deadpans in the voice-over. "I'd flip through catalogs and wonder, *What kind of dining set defines me as a person?*" Later, after a freak accident (or not) obliterates his apartment, he finds himself on the phone with a police investigator, and he whimpers over the fate of his scorched appurtenances. "That condo was my *life*," he says. "I loved every stick of furniture in that place!"

In *Being John Malkovich*, it is John Cusack—a Gen-X mascot if ever we've been saddled with one—who first appears on-screen in the grips of an existential crisis. Actually, the Cusack *puppet* appears first. Cusack plays a frustrated puppeteer named Craig Schwartz, and the opening scene of the movie is a run-through of Craig's marionette magnum opus, "Craig's Dance of Despair and Disillusionment," in which the Cusack puppet breaks a mirror and rubs his hands on his forehead with the sort of histrionics we've come to know from Russian novels. A few moments later, Craig's crashed out in bed, sleeping late, slacking, when his wife, played by Cameron Diaz, tries to rouse him with a gentle jab about maybe, um, you know, *getting a real job*. "Honey, we've been over this," Cusack says. "Nobody's looking for a puppeteer in today's wintry economic climate."

X

It's pretty obvious: both the Edward Norton character and the John Cusack character want to be someone else. Norton is stuck in a feedback loop of yuppie drudgery. Cusack is like a slacker scarab trapped in bohemian amber—here's a guy who is committed to the most marginalized of art forms (puppets!), and the world has chosen to ignore him, and time is running out. Both Cusack and Diaz figure out how to free themselves by becoming John Malkovich. "Everything made sense!" Diaz says, all flushed after being spit out on the side of the New Jersey Turnpike. "I knew who I was!" She and John Cusack achieve their personal transmogrification by fluming down a gloppy tunnel into Malkovich's brain. Edward Norton solves the problem, as it were, by becoming Brad Pitt, and then getting into a series of fistfights with him. Or with himself. It's complicated.

Anyway, in a *New York Times Magazine* profile of that Ray-Banned boomer pasha Jack Nicholson, the writer Ron Rosenbaum said that Nicholson often chooses the movies he wants to make by giving some thought to the ripples that each role could create in American society. Nicholson, Rosenbaum explained, "believes 'the actor is the *litterateur* of his era,' meaning that the actor is capable of 'writing,' even shaping the inner history of his age through his choice of roles and how he plays them." That sounds like utter stoner bullshit, I know, but it's true that if you track each of Nicholson's choices at the height of his impact—*Easy Rider* in 1969, *Five Easy Pieces* in 1970, *Carnal Knowledge* in 1971, *The Last Detail* in 1973, *Chinatown* in 1974, *The Passenger* and *One Flew Over the Cuckoo's Nest* in 1975—you can see all that boomer idealism about peace and love gradually hardening into cynicism and disillusionment.

And I think you can draw similar conclusions from *Being John Malkovich* and *Fight Club*. I think it's more than a fluke of the Hollywood release schedule that both of these movies came out in 1999—a year when the dot-com elixir was spilling over the sides of the goblet, a year when a millennial mall rat named Britney Spears was hammering the final spike into the coffin of alternative rock, a year when the Next Seattle turned out to be your computer screen, a year when Gen X could no longer muster up much of a resistance to the delights of the almighty dollar.

"Do you see what a metaphysical can of worms this portal is?" Cusack says after floating around for a while in John Malkovich's gray matter. "I don't see how I could go on living my life the way I've lived it before."

2. IDIOTS RULE
2000–2006: SUCKING

The Decline of Adulthood

In the New History, nothing was judged—only counted. The power of judging was then subtracted from what it was necessary for a man to learn to do. In the New History, the preferences of a child carried as much weight as the preferences of an adult. . . .

—*George W. S. Trow*, Within the Context of No Context

Greetings, citizens. We are living in the age in which the pursuit of all values other than money, success, fame, glamour has either been discredited or destroyed.

—*Narrator on Felix da Housecat's "Money, Success, Fame, Glamour," popular in nightclubs early in the twenty-first century*

I wish I was like you
Easily amused

—*Nirvana, "All Apologies"*

We heard it off in the distance at first, the flapping and shrieking.

We weren't sure what it was, and we didn't pay attention. We were minding our own business, having finally settled into a comfortable rhythm in our own private Bodega Bay, our sheltered cove, our remote village at the end of the 1990s. It wasn't a real village, but it was home. More than a physical place, it was a *covenant*. An agreement, let's say. It was a vision of American culture that we understood—humane, diverse, passionate, sarcastic, contrary, simultaneously old and new. We took it for granted. We had, in some ways, become complacent, but isn't that the natural progression of things? We knew the neighbors. We knew our way around the streets. We knew where to find a good cup of coffee, a yoga center, a *bellissimo* selection of vintage vinyl, a *gemütlich* bookstore, an *authentique* Belgian bistro that served double-crisped *frites* and frothy goblets of Chimay and stayed open later than it was supposed to. This was where we lived. *Home.* It was, to use the contemporary parlance, sustainable. We figured it would last.

Yes, technology was galloping forward at a manic clip, but we were still young and we felt as though we could keep up with it. "Change is the only constant"—we had internalized the *Fast Company* song-and-dance by now. We were fluent in corporate jargon. We had skill sets; we had 401(k)s; we had 529s. Nobody tarred and feathered us with the word *slacker* anymore. In fact, *because* we were Xers, because we were people who were said to have both a loafer's love of freedom and a lizard-eyed respect for commerce, it was believed that we were uniquely trained for twenty-first-century combat. Maybe we were stoned, but that only made us better at multitasking. It helped us see the big picture. We were the new model. We had heads full of data. We were just getting started. We were poised to make sure—finally, for once—that American culture did not suck.

And that's when we heard the gulls.

Squawk squawk squawk squawk squawk squawk . . .

They sounded innocent at first. Sweet, even. We barely noticed.

"Oh look, honey. There, over the harbor. Those birds . . ."

"Hmmm. Yeah. Wow, there certainly are a lot of them. What are they doing?"

"I don't know. It looks like some kind of feeding frenzy."

Swooping and diving, swooping and diving. A darkening sky.

Squawk squawk squawk squawk squawk squawk . . .

The neighbors stepped out to take a look. What had been nothing more than a tiny, swooping cloudlet looked bigger now. It gathered over the bay like a thunderhead. You couldn't hear yourself think. All you could hear was that flock of birds, and these birds had a *language*. They could talk. They could not, in fact, *stop* talking. As the gulls flapped and shrieked closer and closer to Main Street, it became clear that the noise they produced was more than a squawk. No, you could make out the words now—just before a claw autographed a little scrape across your cheek:

OMIGOD OMIGOD OMIGOD OMIGOD OMIGOD OMIGOD OMIGOD OMIGOD OMIGOD . . .

X

In the worlds of forestry, farming, and computer programming, insiders often talk about the perils of a monoculture. When you have a monoculture, you have one system or substance that is so dominant—pine trees, corn, potatoes, Microsoft—that nothing else can flourish. A monoculture, like any kind of corporate monopoly, is a great way to maximize profits, but it's a bad way to maintain a fertile environment. Diversity withers. Soil is sapped. Certain nutrients are drained from the earth without being replenished. If a disease emerges and wipes out the entire crop of corn or potatoes, you've got nothing left.

It is far too simplistic, and usually wrong, to say that Xers are still ambivalent about getting rich. I don't know any Xers who haven't, in one odd way or another, embraced their inner capitalist by now. Most of us are pragmatic enough to realize that without seed money you don't have independent publishing houses or Internet start-ups or philanthropy or food. But if there is one thing that Xers *are* temperamentally opposed to, it's a monoculture. A monoculture is a lot like Milan Kundera's concept of "totalitarian kitsch," and everything that appeals to the X sensibility—in music, in technology, in design, in enterprise—tends to run counter to that. If X is anything, it's a challenge to the very idea of a cartel. Let's say the monoculture is Phil Collins in his "Sussudio" phase. In that case the Replacements are the blight, the aphid, the phylloxera that reveals the barrenness of the monoculture. For a while we thought we had licked it, but by the beginning of the twenty-first century, the monoculture had come roaring back.

If the wonks of pop were taken by surprise when Nirvana's *Nevermind* toppled Michael Jackson in 1992, they got blindsided all over again in 1999 when the *Billboard* chart was conquered, more or less out of the blue, by a midriff-baring, Mouseketeering strumpet named Britney Spears. By 1999 the alternative revolution was already a goldfish flopping around on a linoleum floor, but this represented the final gasp. Now the goldfish was getting squished beneath a stiletto heel.

There was no stopping somebody like Britney Spears. Her ambition was total and pure, uncluttered by any of that vacillating weenie stuff about the corporation and art. Art had nothing to do with it. Her music was bubblegum without apologies, and in *that* the monoculture had engineered its revenge. You could see it in the opening frames of the ". . . Baby One More Time" video, which, just like the "Smells Like Teen Spirit" video, took place in a high school. There was Britney sitting in a classroom, tapping her black shoe against the leg of a desk, twiddling her pencil, bored out of her pigtailed skull. Some frumpy, four-eyed teacher was lecturing about the Constitution or Emily Dickinson or, *like, whatever,* but when the 3:00 p.m. bell pealed out the chimes of freedom, Britney and a squadron of nymphets went tumbling into the hallway to dance. They danced by the lockers and they danced in a sunny parking lot. They wrapped things up by dancing in a gymnasium.

It would be fatuous to use pop videos as a way to illustrate the evolution of an entire decade in American culture, so let's go ahead and do it. If you want to understand what happened to the X sensibility in the nineties, everything starts with the gym scene in "Smells Like Teen Spirit," and everything ends with the gym scene in ". . . Baby Onc More Time." Those are the bookends. The fun part of the Nirvana video was that it disintegrated into a soup of banging heads and flailing limbs. The Britney video did not disintegrate at all, and that's what was new and interesting about it. These kids had no interest in anarchy. Their dancing was orderly and regimented, with just the sort of goose-steppy punctilio that had gone out of fashion eight years earlier.

"Yes, there's a revolution under way among today's kids—a *good news revolution,*" demographers Neil Howe and William Strauss would write in 2000 in *Millennials Rising: The Next Great Generation,* barely containing their glee. "This generation is going to rebel by behaving not worse, but *better.* Their life mission will not be to tear down old institutions that don't work, but to build up new ones that do. Look closely at youth indicators, and you'll see that *Millennial attitudes and behaviors represent a sharp break from Generation X, and are running exactly counter to trends launched by the Boomers.*" Those are not my italics, by the way. They're in the book. Howe and Strauss must have been really excited about this. Like Humbert Humbert ogling Lolita in her kneesocks and saddle shoes, they go on to rave about how these super-duper millennials are optimists! Who accept authority! And follow rules! *Oh, happy happy, joy joy.*

Lemminglike and Abercrombie & Fitched, these new kids cared about belonging, they cared about *the group.* They did everything in groups, they even dated in groups. They moved in noisy little packs, they only read books if there was a book club with which to share them, they networked, they sought out mentors, they kept each other in line. They wanted to connect with everyone; they wanted the world to cuddle up with them on Friendster and Facebook. They were unfamiliar with the notion of privacy. Solitude made them . . . uncomfortable. To be private was not to belong, and to be alone was to hear yourself think, and they didn't like that. But that was okay because that's what cell phones and Black-Berries were for, to keep you from having to, *like, oh my God*, think for more than thirty seconds. Like their parents, the boomers, there was nothing they revered more than the hive.

Such was their groupthink that they didn't even mind if you called it groupthink. They agreed. They agreed that they all agreed. An Xer would be insulted; a millennial took pride in it. And when the marketing scouts started to pick up on this seismic activity, on this huge and happy transcontinental tribe that responded correctly to every cue, well, joy washed through the corner offices.

For their good behavior the millennials would be rewarded with treats. "There's never been more attention paid to a specific generation," music journalist Dave Adelson told *USA Today* in 2000. "This generation has a voracious appetite, and the record companies are happy to satiate it. Kids are being bombarded with more and more types of media designed for their demographic, with some marketing plans targeting 5-year-olds." With all this going on, it probably should not have come as a shock that Xers—always so *difficult*, always making those marketing executives climb the walls—began to fall out of favor. "Generation X has been kicked to the curb," said Alan Light, then the editor in chief of *Spin*. "They look like chumps." It might be helpful to think of this cultural passage as the Skipping Point: you know you've become a full-fledged adult when it dawns on you that MTV doesn't love you anymore.

It made sense that MTV loved the new kids, because the new kids were obedient. Their prototype was Tracy Flick, the Reese

Witherspoon character in the movie *Election*—so ruthlessly goody-two-shoes, so out-of-bed-early-and-determined-to-win, that everyone else looked like a mewling sad sack in comparison. Millennials made their parents proud. "Their connection to their parents is deep and strong," Middlebury College psychology professor Barbara Hofer told *Newsweek*. "They say, 'My parents are my best friends.' People would have seen that as aberrant a generation ago, as pathological." Meanwhile the parents, having spent years and fortunes training their plum offspring with the sort of iron rigor previously reserved for Soviet gymnasts, could only look on and applaud—oh, dear, yet another perfect 10! "And so I can predict with what I believe is considerable accuracy this about the century to come," gushed the boomer soothsayer Anna Quindlen. "It will be remarkable because its history will be shaped, and written, too, by a group of what promises to be remarkable human beings. The millennials, demographers have named them, born between 1977 and 1994, 70 million strong, the biggest bump in our national line graph since their parents, the baby boomers. These are our children; for my money they are a great bunch. My three are simply better than I was at their age. They are more interesting, more confident, less hidebound and uptight, better educated, more creative and, in some essential fashion, unafraid. We can say with pride that some of that is because of the world we have created for them."

Pick Flick!

In August 2006, *Women's Wear Daily* published an item about the shift in focus at *Jane*, the magazine—originally founded by *Sassy* goddess Jane Pratt—that had been aimed at women who had an equal interest in PJ Harvey and Prada. *Jane* had a new editor, Brandon Holley, and she was perceptive enough to notice a mutation in the readership. "In part," *WWD* put it, "the sell has been about sociological changes in twentysomething women since *Jane*'s heyday (the zeitgeist having gone from 'antiestablishment/angry/slackers' to 'pretty/fun/optimistic,' according to *Jane*'s market research), plus the so-called Gen-Y population boomlet that provides more potential readers. Holley called the transition a shift from 'cooler than thou' to 'I make it cool.'" Recognition of that shift might've come a little too late; *Jane* went out of business in the summer of 2007.

One day, a press release happened to cross my desk. This is how it began:

> I am proud to announce the formation of a new fashion public relations firm, Big Bad Wolf Communications.
>
> My name is Jason Wolf and I am a 21-year-old risk taker who has finally bid farewell to coffee runs and intern mailings to represent a prestigious and diverse collection of clothing lines listed below.

X

Ronald Reagan was the first president they even remembered, and it became common to say that the millennials were the most conservative generation since the 1950s, but that didn't mean that you could pick up an explicit strain of right-wing dogma in their favorite music and TV shows. Teen-pop performers like Britney Spears, 'N Sync, and the Backstreet Boys acted more like ideological drug mules: they looked so innocent that you wouldn't suspect them of anything, and *that*, in effect, became the message. The status quo was baked right into the music. If Gen-X music tended to sound as though it came from a specific place—Seattle or Manchester, Compton or Minneapolis or the South Bronx—the new millennial soundtrack came across as geographically blank. It didn't merely sound like something you would *buy* at Wal-Mart, it sounded like Wal-Mart itself: cheap, clean, massive, censored, and generic.

The only rebellious thing about teen-pop performers like Britney Spears, 'N Sync, and the Backstreet Boys was their explicit distaste for rebellion. In the summer of 1999 Jon Pareles wrote in the *New York Times* that "kiddie-pop's top acts present the image of extremely good children: ambitious and diligent and virtuous. The

CD-ROM component of Britney Spears's album, '. . . Baby One More Time,' includes a photo scrapbook of her training and triumphs: dance class, gymnastics trophies, her selection at age 10 as Miss Talent USA. She's not just a superkid. She's obedient, too, singing the songs and hitting the marks that are choreographed for her. So do the boy groups, synchronizing their moves without a trace of mischief. Pop provides wish-fulfillment for listeners, and kiddie pop can give adults the ultimate parental fantasy: well-groomed, perfectly behaved, highly motivated adolescents who—fantasy of fantasies—always do as they're told."

Of course, all this was before Britney would segue into shaving her head, floating in and out of rehab, eschewing undergarments, freaking out on airplanes, and tooling around with unbuckled infants in her lap, but even later, even as she downward-spiraled into the zone of totally bat-shit behavior, she could be counted on to do what was expected of her. Miss Talent USA remained fiercely obedient to fame. If the cameras were around, she did their bidding.

The millennial stars were all business. There would be no Eddie Vedder–style going-into-hiding nonsense for them. Families were brands, and brands needed to be built upon, nurtured, maximized. Britney Spears had a sister, Jamie Lynn. Jessica Simpson had a sister, Ashlee. Paris Hilton had a sister, Nicky. Nick Carter from the Backstreet Boys had a brother, Aaron. These siblings could be used as ancillary profit centers. Synergies could be developed. In 2000 only three acts—the Backstreet Boys, 'N Sync, and Britney Spears—moved an astonishing 31 million units for Jive Records. Two years later Backstreet brother Aaron Carter grossed something in the neighborhood of $7 million from fifty concerts. "We still came in with a decent-sized profit, but I would say the numbers were somewhat down," his manager told *Billboard*. "We're taking a little break with Aaron to look at film and TV projects. We're co-producing a sitcom for Aaron next year, with big interest from UPN, ABC Family, and WB. We need a venue to reach Aaron's market, and TV is a good way to do that. I'm in control of this career, and I'm making sure to branch out to different mediums." His manager happened to be his mother, Jane Carter. At the time, Aaron Carter was fourteen.

X

In comparison to the Tracy Flick shock troops, Xers were a generation of Prufrocks, forever hesitating before making the leap; a generation of Salieris, now resentfully squeezed in between two gaudy, explosive, and taboo-smashing Mozarts. Standards? Quality? Tradition? The prototypical millennial didn't seem to give a rat's ass about words like that, just as he couldn't give a rat's ass that I just made pretentious references to T. S. Eliot and *Amadeus*. The new millennial heroes—Jessica Simpson, Paris Hilton, Lindsay Lohan, Kevin Federline, Brody Jenner—were embraced not for doing anything well, per se, but simply for doing a lot: for hustling and for hiring publicists and agents who were skilled at cranking that hustle into an eternally returning melodrama of curiosity. Having smashed the old concepts of stardom to smithereens, these "Page Six" fixtures had no aspirations other than to make the world care about their perpetual play, and to make a fortune from that, and to use said fortune to acquire great gobs of high-end swag. Bring on the gift bags! Douglas Coupland had heard them chattering their way toward us all the way back in 1992, when he'd explored the world of a Reaganite "global teen" named Tyler Johnson in the novel *Shampoo Planet*:

> "Mom, go worship your crystals. Poverty blows. I'm not letting poverty happen to me."
> "What makes you think money is so hot, anyway, Tyler?"
> "If money isn't so great, then why do rich people keep it all to themselves?"
> "Maybe being poor for a while would do you good."
> I mute the TV to command her full attention. "Earth to mother. Earth to mother. Poor people eat lousy food. They

smoke. Their houses never have trees. They have too many
kids and they're always surrounded by crying babies. . . ."

If a global teen had to suck to make it, so be it. Sucking was fine.
Sucking was beside the point. "A lot of real young people out there
are being spoon-fed garbage," Richard Patrick, the front man in the
alternative rock band Filter, complained to *USA Today*. "I don't trust
anyone who doesn't write their own songs. I think kids will want
something real next, someone who writes, produces, and sings.
When we make music, it's our baby. That's what's missing in this
corporate teen stuff. They take some kid from the *Mickey Mouse
Show*, teach her to dance a little, add a little hip-hop beat and have a
hit. By the time she's 25, she's going straight downhill freaked out
on too much Xanax." Andy Rooney couldn't have said it better.

Could Jessica Simpson act or sing? Sure. Maybe. Why? Did it
matter? Merely to ask the question was to reveal your fuddy-duddy
Gen-X vestments to the world. "What, like, OMG, you actually
care about *acting* and *singing*, old man?" (As a comparative case
study, consider renting *Reality Bites*, the 1994 movie that was made
to tap the Gen-X fever. Winona Ryder plays a flat-broke documentary filmmaker. Ben Stiller plays a shady MTV-style executive.
Stiller buys a heap of Winona's footage so that he can cut it up,
dumb it down, and put it on TV as a cartoonish reality-based soap
opera. How prescient! But Winona throws a hissy fit because the
suits have ruined the integrity of her work. How quaint!) The new
world of Gawker and Defamer and *Us Weekly* and *American Idol*
and *Laguna Beach* was a fascinating one, to be sure, but it was no
place for a guy who didn't have the guts to part with his vinyl copy
of *Fables of the Reconstruction*.

X

Vast numbers of Generation Xers learned all their moral lessons
from a single source: the 1971 film version of *Willy Wonka & the*

Chocolate Factory. Although the movie was supposedly a bomb when it first came out, it has, over time, grown into an influential work of art. I think I've seen it about a hundred times, and in my years as a journalist the subject of *Willy Wonka & the Chocolate Factory* has come up in more interviews than I can count. I once spent an evening hanging out with Marilyn Manson at his house in the Hollywood Hills. He, too, was obsessed with it.

If you go back and watch *Willy Wonka & the Chocolate Factory* now, it tells you not only everything you need to know about what Xers believe in, but everything you need to know about why Xers find the millennials so exasperating and cracked. We don't need to regurgitate the entire plot here—I'm guessing you know it—but, in short, *Willy Wonka & the Chocolate Factory* concerns five children who get the chance, as part of a worldwide contest and publicity stunt, to spend a day visiting the secret psychedelic chambers of the Wonka candy empire. One of the children is good. His name is Charlie Bucket, and we know that he is good not only because he delivers newspapers to support his impoverished family but because *he does not sell out.* As soon as Charlie finds a Golden Ticket that will allow him to tour the Wonka complex, he is approached by Mr. Slugworth, who exudes a distinct Nazi-war-criminal vibe. Mr. Slugworth tells Charlie the same thing that he's been telling all the kids. He'll reward him with a heap of money if Charlie, while visiting Wonka Inc., will do one simple thing: steal a single Everlasting Gobstopper—the killer app of all candies, and still being tinkered with in Wonka's R&D department—so that Slugworth can rip off the secret formula. Charlie, of course, would *never consider doing such a thing.* Charlie Bucket is Kid A. Charlie is where X begins.

But the other kids? The other kids are rotten to the core. The other kids are mall rats and superbrats, and their behavior represents a tapestry of tawdry conduct. There's Mike Teavee, who's irrationally obsessed with appearing on television. There's Violet

Beauregarde, a hypercompetitive Tracy Flick prototype who is willing to elbow everyone else out of the way in her quest to *win-win-win*. There's Augustus Gloop, a lederhosen-wearing fatty who gobbles up everything in his path. And there is, most tellingly, the heiress Veruca Salt—a princessy preteen harridan who has every intention of handing over an Everlasting Gobstopper to Mr. Slugworth, and whose shrieking catchphrase *"I want it NOW!"* will end up, thirty years later, becoming nothing less than a mission statement for the millennials.

So here's the thing: In *Willy Wonka & the Chocolate Factory*, the four bad kids are *punished*. They suffer. They shrink, swell up, fall down holes, almost drown in chocolate rivers. And you want them to suffer—they deserve it. Charlie Bucket, on the other hand, is rewarded for his honorable behavior: he inherits the candy factory. I saw this movie roughly four or five times a year when I was a kid, as did millions of Xers, if my unscientific analysis is correct. I don't think it's going out on a limb to suggest that repeated absorption of these lessons—it's wrong to sell out, it's wrong to want to be the center of attention, it's wrong to be too grasping and transparent in your ambitions—made a deep and lasting imprint on the Gen-X sensibility.

This might explain, in part, why the millennials were grating on us so much at the beginning of the century. The millennials seemed to revel in doing exactly what the bad Wonka kids did—who were Paris Hilton and Clay Aiken other than updated models of Veruca Salt and Mike Teavee?—and yet they were not punished at all. They were rewarded. America loved them. Theirs was the infinite jest. Their amusements stretched all the way from Orlando to Burbank like an expanse of monocultural starch. And where did that put Generation X? Well, we were left to look on—not unlike Wonka himself, as played so brilliantly by Gene Wilder—muttering our sarcastic asides and waiting for the brats to self-destruct.

I Am Special, I Am Special, Look at Me

The hallmark of the new celebrity—and the wanna-wanna genera-tion that embraced it—was not achievement but willingness. Tal-ent would only serve as an obstruction. What mattered was that the wanna-wannas were willing, in a way that Xers like Kurt Co-bain and Lauryn Hill had not been, to push the art of selling them-selves to any necessary extreme. "Always tell everyone what they want to hear," advises Paris Hilton in her best-selling how-to book, *Confessions of an Heiress*. "Then do what you want. That way, no one ever gets mad at you. They get very confused, then blame it on themselves." There was no such thing as overexposure; the idea of shutting off a cell phone became incomprehensible. If someone wanted you, you were available. Perhaps the signature scene in *1 Night in Paris*, the notorious sex tape that turned Paris Hilton into a global brand, is the one in which she interrupts the rapture of coitus to answer the phone.

If you had the misfortune of appearing in a sex tape, you might be prompted to leave the country, change your name, and pursue, as penance, a lifetime of labor as a fishmonger in Vladivostok. Such an approach was now obsolete. When the Paris Hilton sex tape made the rounds, she assuaged her shame with an outburst of en-terprise. "If the media plays with you, well, play with them," she ruminates in *Confessions of an Heiress*. "I went on *Saturday Night Live* soon after my name was in the headlines every day for something I wasn't too proud of, and which had really upset my family. On 'Weekend Update' with Jimmy Fallon, the script had him asking me, 'Is it hard to get a room in the Paris Hilton? Is it roomy?' and he wanted to cut it. But I wouldn't let him. No way. That was the fun-niest line. And I got the upper hand with the media the moment he said it on national TV. That's when it all clicked and things started to change. People knew I could laugh at myself, and that one bad incident was not going to make me lock myself in my room."

It is often said of Paris Hilton that she is famous for doing nothing, but it must be pointed out that she does a great deal of nothing. Her ever-expanding empire includes a line of lingerie and sportswear, energy drinks, wigs, books, dance music CDs, and a hit reality show on TV, *The Simple Life*. Should you feel compelled to buy *Paris*, her fizzled shot at pop stardom, the first thing you'll see when you open up the CD case is an advertisement: a little insert flutters out like a sparrow, and on it there are plugs for Paris ringtones, Paris watches, the Paris Hilton Handbag Collection, and Heiress, the Paris Hilton fragrance. "I found out I like working," she observes in her book. "It makes you appreciate things more. So, even if people say I'm spoiled, at least they can't say I don't do anything. When they see me at parties now, they know it's probably for a reason. Now I have an agenda like everybody else."

X

On February 27, 2007, the *Los Angeles Times* published a story about a study that had been undertaken by Jean Twenge, a psychologist and associate professor at San Diego State University. The title of the study was "Egos Inflating Over Time," and it took a look at the remarkable surge in narcissism among members of the millennial generation. Paris Hilton might strike you as little more than a fluky and opportunistic media succubus, but based on what Professor Twenge and her colleagues discovered, Paris is merely the most successful example of a new American mind-set. More than sixteen thousand college students had filled out psychological surveys, and the blowback had left Professor Twenge feeling "very, very worried," as the *Times* reported:

> The Narcissistic Personality Inventory asks students to react to such statements as: "If I ruled the world, it would be a better place," "I think I am a special person" and "I like to be the center of attention."

The study found that almost two-thirds of recent college students had narcissism scores that were above the average 1982 score. Thirty percent more college students showed elevated narcissism in 2006 than in 1982. . . .

Some of the increase in narcissistic attitudes was probably caused by the self-esteem programs that many elementary schools adopted 20 years ago, the study suggests. It notes that nursery schools began to have children sing songs that proclaim: "I am special, I am special. Look at me."

Other trends in American culture, including permissive parenting, increased materialism and the fascination with celebrities and reality TV shows, may also heighten self-regard, said study coauthor W. Keith Campbell, psychology professor at the University of Georgia. "It's part of a whole cultural system," he said.

We'll Make Great Pets

If the mainstream changes, the criticism of it has to change too; which is to say that the oppositional or ironic attitude, the counter-attitude, must change. I am very interested in counter-attitudes. They are absolutely necessary ingredients in culture. If those attitudes are not present, any culture becomes a form of lobotomization.

—*Susan Sontag, 1988, interviewed in Sweden by Stefan Jonsson*

When Janice Min was growing up in Colorado, her father made his living for a while as a professor of zoology. He worked with small laboratory animals—rats, turtles, hamsters, rabbits, guinea pigs— and he would periodically bring a furry critter home so that his daughter would have a pet. Before long, the pet would vanish—

whisked back to the dissection chamber in the name of science. She got used to this.

It's tempting to observe that Janice Min has brought the same aptitude for emotional detachment to her professional life. She is the editor in chief of *Us Weekly*, the crown jewel of the celebrity glossies, where *Rolling Stone* suzerain Jann Wenner pays her more than a million dollars a year to chronicle the couplings and canoodlings, breakups and breakdowns of the barely housebroken creatures who've come to dominate what's left of our popular culture. Paris, Lindsay, Britney, Britney, Lindsay, Paris—if their names loop around and around in the mass mind with the bubblegummy relentlessness of an Oscar Mayer jingle, well, it is Min's job to *keep* that happening, to prevent the tune from ever dropping out of the American headspace.

And yet her interest in the plumage and mating rituals of these curious beasts is primarily clinical. Outside of her job, she has no burning interest in celebrities. She never has. She didn't read the teen magazines back in Colorado. She was a civics geek. She devoured the op-ed page of the newspaper. She could tick off the names of every member of the presidential cabinet. Okay, she did love R.E.M.—she used to play *Murmur* over and over, basking in its jangly Gregorian rapture—but, by now, nearing forty, with a husband and two kids, she admits to having stopped caring about music. "We were talking about it at the office yesterday," she says, making her way through a plate of chicken teriyaki at the back table of a Japanese restaurant in midtown Manhattan. "R.E.M. just got inducted into the Rock and Roll Hall of Fame. I don't think a band like R.E.M. could really exist now. They're just too—I don't know—they're not attractive."

Min has an affectless voice. She went to high school in Littleton, the same town that produced the Columbine killers, and her accent, like the clipped cadence of a teleprompter reader on a cable news show, is shorn of any regional characteristics.

She could, like *Us Weekly* itself, be from anywhere. Listen closely, though, and you can figure out her cultural coordinates.

She has a Big-Media accent. It's there in the way she delivers the word "yeah." She says "yeah" in much the same way that Andy Warhol used to say "wow." (And as art critic Mark Stevens once put it, "Warhol's 'wow' is almost too complicated to translate.") It's a "yeah" that mimics the feeling of enthusiasm and sponges it away at the same time. If you're having a conversation with Janice Min and you begin to hazard an observation about something in American life, you're likely to hear that Big-Media "yeah" before you're halfway through the sentence.

There's nothing abrupt or rude about this. It sounds, at first, like the "yeah" of affirmation: *Yes, I am listening; I confirm what you are saying; please keep going.* But the more contact you have with Janice Min's "yeah," the more you realize that the sound of it resembles the spasm of a dying fish. At the beginning of the "yeah" is a sharp intake of breath, and at the end, with the "ah," there is a languorous, downward flap of the tail.

That last part seems to say: *Yes, I know, I know, I've heard it all before; I am incapable of surprise or outrage.*

Running *Us Weekly* might seem like an easy job, even rudimentary—I mean, just splash a bunch of paparazzi photos across the page and candy up the headlines with Easter-eggy dustings of pink and yellow and purple—but as Min can tell you, it's more complicated than that. It involves nuance, clairvoyance, intricacy. It's the Big-Media equivalent of biological taxonomy. You can't fake it. You have to be able to gauge precisely how much Lindsay is *too much* Lindsay, or whether Angelina's latest adventure in Third World infant acquisition registers as *news* or blah redundancy. At *Us Weekly* there can be no mission creep. A shopper who picks up the magazine in the checkout line at the Food Emporium must do so with a sense of faith that he or she is going to thumb through photographs of people who are *supposed* to be photographed. If that shopper were to pick up *Us Weekly* and see a random snapshot of, say, Peter Buck eating a jelly doughnut, it could be confusing. Catastrophic, even. Bonds of trust would have been ruptured. The whole enterprise might collapse. Conversely, if a public figure fails to appear in the magazine for a sustained period of time, a reader should not interpret the vanishing act as accidental. "They cease to be celebrities if they're not in *Us Weekly*," Min says. "They need this. If you aren't covered in *Us Weekly* for a year, you are no longer a celebrity. The greatest disappointment for any celebrity would be to get dressed up, go out, get photographed, and no one runs your photo. That would be—it means it didn't happen."

On the surface Janice Min's line of work may be out of synch with what we might think of as Gen-X principles, but there is something classically X about her trajectory. Ask her what words she tends to associate with Generation X, and she says, with barely a pause, *disappointment*. "You always think that your generation is going to do amazing things," she says. "I feel like I just know a lot of people who ended up just not exactly where they wanted to be." Min herself didn't expect to traffic in trivia. "I almost went to work at the *Wall Street Journal*, way back when. But I look at those areas of journalism right now—they're so dead, they're so moribund," she says. "The dissection of the trivial has taken on this paramount importance, and *Us Weekly* is very proud of its dissection of the trivial. This is what it does. It is escape. It is fun. It is entertainment."

Min moved to New York City for college and graduated from Columbia in 1990, when the recessionary shriveling of the job market was kicking in. Sensibly, she ducked back into school and got a graduate degree in journalism, also from Columbia, a year later. "I thought it was profoundly depressing that a lot of people left jobs to go to journalism school, got themselves in debt, and then left journalism school to no job," she says. "I was one of the lucky few people that did get a job—at a local newspaper, right out of school. But it's funny, money never factored into my thinking. I made, what, twenty-eight thousand dollars a year in my first job, and I never thought I was going to make much more than that." She sees this stoic attitude—work hard, pay your dues, accept your fate—as the opposite of the fizzy entitlement percolating up from the millennial ranks. "I feel like the younger generation today knows so much about salaries and compensation. It amazes me, the gall of some young people. Like, you know, they come in and ask for promotions after six months. There's not one person who works with me who would've ever done my first job—Tuesday through Saturday, covering cops and planning boards and school boards from two o'clock to ten o'clock. Like, that would be personal hell for these young women who get to go to Bungalow 8 and cover red carpets."

If it's odd to hear these observations from the editor in chief of *Us Weekly*, that's because a lot of people see the magazine itself as a symptom of this generational shift in sensibility. You might even say that *Us Weekly* is *responsible* for fostering the impression that there's no higher purpose in life than to be photographed getting hauled off to rehab in a stretch limo after a shopping spree at Kitson.

"The young generation has no critical eye," Min says. It astounds her sometimes, the way the kids coming up insist on turning every private act into a public spectacle. "Why have a birthday party if you're not going to put the photos on MySpace?" she says. "They've all created their own little *Us Weekly* worlds on the Internet." What seems to matter to the prototypical millennial is "being the prettiest, being the thinnest, having the best clothes, having the best handbag, dating the hottest guy."

She goes on. "I'm thirty-seven. I don't really know a lot of people my age who are interested in vast self-promotion. Like, I don't know anyone my age who would've auditioned for a reality show. It's mortifying! MySpace—everyone who's my age says, 'Who in the world would ever do a MySpace page and reveal these intimate details about yourself and try to prove how many friends you have?' That is in *stark* opposition to our generation."

These are mere observations, though—not personal gripes. Listening to Min talk about this stuff, in that bone-dry Big-Media accent of hers, you will detect nothing that might be described as aversion or regret. She is, after all, a scientist. Some species survive when the veldt becomes seedless and parched; some turn into domesticated playmates; others are doomed. The smart ones understand this. They adapt. *They get used to it.* The rest? Well, they're lucky if they end up suspended in jars of formaldehyde. "I don't think there is a counterculture," Min says as a restaurant server whisks away her plate. "When we were young, there were always the faux suburban punk rockers. That doesn't even exist anymore. It's not *cool* to be Daria. It's not cool to be the disaffected youth. I can just imagine all the young people in the office—they would just think that that person's a real downer.

"I don't think anyone really *wants* to be underground. Why would you want to be underground when you can be aboveground and be more successful, more famous, more popular?"

Yeah.

Refugee

> There used to be flea markets by my house where you could buy all sorts of little things. Now it's all Home Depots.
>
> —*Lauryn Hill, in* Rolling Stone, *February 18, 1999*

Imagine a bright, beautiful girl who loves God. Imagine her living in South Orange, New Jersey, and imagine 1975, the year she was born. This is the year that her mother, Valerie, makes a maternal sacrifice. Valerie piles together all the hit singles she's been collecting over the years, the vinyl forty-fives—Stevie Wonder and Aretha Franklin, Marvin Gaye and Gladys Knight and Donny Hathaway—this music as intricate as tapestry, as lubricious as almond oil, and stows it all away in a box in the basement. Now imagine the girl, Lauryn, getting bored one afternoon a few years later and peeking around in that basement and discovering a box full of records.

"One day little Lauryn found 'em," Valerie would tell Touré, a writer from *Rolling Stone*, many years later. "They all came upstairs. And thus began a journey. She started to play that music and loved it. One o'clock in the morning, you'd go into her room and you'd see her fast asleep with the earphones on. The sixties soul that I'd collected just seeped into her veins."

Now imagine that same girl, a lot older, slicing open one of those veins and letting plasma trickle down a microphone stand. That's what it sounds like when she walks into a studio in New York City in the summer of 2001, only a few weeks before the terrorist attack on the World Trade Center. There, in front of a live audience summoned by MTV, Lauryn Hill delivers one of the most cracked performances ever captured on disk. Columbia Records will release it a year later and call it *Unplugged 2.0*. But the mood feels more like *unhinged, uncorked, unnerving*. "I used to get dressed for y'all, now I don't do that no more. I'm sorry. It's a new day. Don't have the energy," Hill starts to say as the audience laughs uncomfortably. "It's real interesting, because I used to be a performer, and I really don't consider myself a performer so much anymore. I'm really just—you know, I'm sharing, you know, more or less, the music that I've been given, but if I stop, if I start, if I, you know, feel like sayin' *baby, baby, baby* for eighteen bars, or whatever, you know, I just—I do that. But, um. All right, so you guys are cool? I'm talkin' to the people in my head, too."

In between finding the vinyl stash in South Orange and going unplugged in 2001, a lot had happened to Lauryn Hill. She'd sold millions of records as a member of the Fugees. Her 1998 solo album, *The Miseducation of Lauryn Hill*, a heady gumbo of Detroit soul and Kingston reggae, South Bronx scratching and Bed-Stuy stoop doo-wop and backseat slow jams, had won five Grammy Awards and redefined the contours of American music. "Black music right now is like this whole *Star Wars* battle," Ahmir "?uestlove" Thompson, the drummer for the Roots, told *Rolling Stone* in 1999. "There are very few people who are on the side of art and are goin' up against the Death Star. D'Angelo is Luke Skywalker. Prince, Stevie, James, Marvin and George are our Yoda and Obi-Wan Kenobi. And, most definitely, Lauryn is Princess Leia."

But something else had happened to Lauryn Hill, too. Something had knocked her off balance. You could hear it there in that studio, in the raggedness of her voice, every time she leaned into the microphone. "I know I'm up here and you know Lauryn Hill and you came to see Lauryn Hill, but this is the first time y'all meetin' me. You see what I'm sayin'? Don't think you met me before. Okay, and as I grow, you're gonna meet me a little bit more, you're going to be exposed to the real me a little bit more. . . . Listen, y'all never knew *me*. I want to introduce you to me. I'm just getting to know me."

She rambled on like this between every song. "Yeah, I'm crazy and deranged, you know, and I'm free. You see? I'm free. I might play you songs and twitch a little bit, just so people know. Look, I'm tellin' you, when they think you're crazy, they don't mess with you. I'm *tellin'* you. Y'all think that's a curse. I'ma tell you, it's a blessing. It's a *blessing*. When I was a politician, boy, everybody was just all over me. You know, I didn't have a private moment at all. Not one private moment. Now that people think I'm crazy and deranged, we have peace. Total peace."

It didn't sound like peace. Something—the artificiality of show business, the pressure of trying to follow up a masterpiece, way too little sleep, too much idle chitchat with the people in her head—had broken her spirit. Now, she said, she'd "retired from a fantasy." She was sick of the stress, sick of image maintenance, sick of "monotonous ritual," sick of "slavin'." More than anything, she was sick of being disconnected from the treasure chest that she'd dug up in that basement in South Orange. "Music was my love, and because of everything I thought had to accompany my music, it became my burden," she told the dumbstruck crowd that day. "It just got stolen from me. I said, 'What is this? How did this thing that I love so much so easily and so quickly turn into something I loathe and hate?'"

I bring this up because Lauryn Hill's psychic suffering at that *Unplugged* concert stands in glaring contrast to the gleeful suckitude that was so plentiful in pop music at the dawn of the twenty-first century. Just as the *Miseducation* phenomenon was cresting, in 1998, Hill told *Entertainment Weekly* that her goal was to serve people juicy homemade burgers even though they'd gotten used to the assembly-line patties at McDonald's. But within a few months of her saying that, the assembly line went full tilt. The new breed of pop tarts—Britney Spears, Christina Aguilera, Jessica Simpson, Mandy Moore—seemed to have been put together by an R&D wunderkind at the Barbie factory, some *Starship Troopers*–style artificial-intelligence renegade with a fetish for Scandinavoid teen pop and bottle-blond fembots. The music had a *clank* to it: If you couldn't differentiate one hit single from another, or even one singer from another, that's because you weren't supposed to. They were, in sound and spirit, identical. The music of Britney Spears and the Backstreet Boys was engineered to be the opposite of homemade and juicy. It spoke to you of big-box stores and synthetic trans fats, of robotic porn and Pokémon.

It had nothing to do with some musty cellar full of musical history. Instead, it replicated a successful business model straight out of—weirdly enough—the Kinko's Lacuna. Color Me Badd and New Kids on the Block begat the Backstreet Boys and 'N Sync. Mariah Carey and Paula Abdul begat Christina Aguilera and Britney Spears. (And later, more distressingly, Green Day begat Blink 182, Sum 41, and Good Charlotte, bands that aped the chord progressions and the sullen-brat vocal timbres of punk rock without bothering to give their songs a hint of iconoclastic purpose.) The trilling vocal gymnastics, the synchronized breakin'-in-Białystok dance moves, the beats that sounded like new jack swing remixed for a luxury brothel in Reno, the sticky hair, the shiny sweatpants—it was as though somebody had siphoned a whole bunch of signifiers right out of 1990 and mulched them into the ground beef served in and around Orlando, Florida. Lauryn was right. It was hard to wean people off fast food.

As for her existential crisis, nobody wanted to hear about it. Caring about music had become dreadfully unfashionable. Claiming not to care about your public image had become incomprehensible—anyone who said stuff like this *had* to be nuts, right? Princess Leia's *Unplugged 2.0* bombed. It didn't even bomb—that would imply that there were expectations behind it. *Unplugged 2.0* failed to penetrate the national consciousness in the slightest way. Nobody noticed. In the span of four years Lauryn Hill had gone from being one of the most important new voices in American culture—beaming out from the cover of *Time*—to the show business equivalent of a bag lady hectoring a street lamp.

The Grand March

> These are dangerous days
> To say what you feel is to dig your own grave
>
> —*Sinéad O'Connor, "Black Boys on Mopeds"*

Oh, there were thousands of ways you could rationalize it, explain it, come up with theories about it, find buried meaning in it, *contextualize* it, especially if you happened to have an advanced degree from Brown University and had spent a little time soaking your brain in a vat of metonymy and synecdoche, paradigmatic and syntagmatic relations, and MTV queer theory. The point of all that clotted and impenetrable academic language was that nothing was good and nothing was bad, it was all just *text* waiting to be picked apart like a rotisserie chicken. By the end of the twentieth century, the semiotics scholars and the corporate marketing strategists were reduced to saying the same thing: *It doesn't matter. Just put it out there. Just sell it.* The "soul" people—they were a bad investment, anyway. You couldn't count on them. They didn't stick to the contract. Look at the music world. The artists were always dying or going mad, or both. Kurt Cobain offs himself. Jeff Buckley drowns in the Mississippi River. Elliott Smith shoves a dagger into his own chest. Tupac and Biggie get gunned down. Sinéad O'Connor makes one lunatic proclamation after another. Lauryn Hill wins Grammys and then decides the whole celebrity industry is a vicious lie. No, you couldn't have artists acting like that. It was bad for business. It screwed with the five-year plans and the quarterly reports. You invested in these people and then they imploded. It was like too much turnover in a branch office; it fucked with the budget to keep retraining people.

This is why *American Idol* was so perfect—an example of totalitarian kitsch at its most sophisticated. *American Idol* weeded out the freaks and churned out consistent, if uninspired, product. The demented original, the visionary loon—those kinds of contestants were doomed from the get-go. Simon Cowell would march them into the studio for the tryouts, mock them, and send them packing. The message was: *Get with the program.* The objective was obedience. Winning the *American Idol* competition meant that (1) you were, by virtue of having survived the process, willing to get with the program, and (2) the people who bought pop records already liked you, because they had voted for you, so they would buy more of you as long as you didn't change. Of course, you couldn't go around referring to *American Idol* as "totalitarian kitsch" or you'd never get invited to cocktail parties. Slagging on *American Idol* was like slagging on candy. The second you wagged your finger at it, you'd turned yourself into the Most Tedious Dentist in the World, yammering on about how sugar rots the teeth. *Yeah yeah yeah, totalitarian kitsch, whatever . . .*

What this cultural system seemed intent on rubbing out was the idea of soul. *Soul*, in fact, became one of those words that you weren't supposed to use anymore. It was semiotic poison. If we take, as a guide, some of the definitions of *soul* that I can find here in the small dictionary on my desk, we're talking about "the principle of life, feeling, and thought, in humans, regarded as a distinct spiritual entity separate from the body," along with a "noble warmth of spirit" and "the inspirer of some action." It's safe to say that the media bombardments of the twenty-first-century monoculture had nothing to do with that. It is also true that we shouldn't jump to conclusions about human behavior simply because of the epidemic popularity of reality shows, social networking sites, and superficial pop stars, but to think about concepts like "noble warmth" and "spiritual entity separate from the body" in connection with, say, the Paris Hilton Handbag Collection is to get a bracing sense of what's been lost.

Consider that "inspirer of some action" part. If we're using music as an example, the songs of Nirvana and Public Enemy, Lauryn Hill and Radiohead, Mary J. Blige and Jeff Buckley are soulful because of the presence of genuine and messy human qualities embedded in the music itself—love, anger, ache, torpor, fleeting transcendence, guilt, repentance, lunacy, a feeling of joyful release from bondage, et cetera—but they are also soulful because of what they inspire. They inspire you to pay attention, to wake up, to question your surroundings, to recognize and maybe even fight for the integrity of your interior life. Mostly, they just acknowledge the *existence* of that interior life, whereas the music favored in mass numbers by the wanna-wanna consumer had no purpose other than to encourage you to buy more stuff. It provided a soundtrack for shopaholics. The music wasn't so much "music" as it was an audio advertisement for a new product that happened to be shelved in the music department. The purpose of the music was to sell more of the product. There's nothing ethically wrong about selling more of a product—I'm as susceptible as the next guy to the beguiling charms of a cheesy pop song—but what began to grate, in the infant years of the twenty-first century, was the all-encompassing monopoly of the sell. You couldn't get away from the sell, and that meant that almost any form of artistic expression that *did* spring up from that old-fashioned notion of soul was so marginalized as to become invisible.

If we're willing to talk about soul, if we're willing to risk being that severely uncool, if we are willing to consider emotions like love and heartache and rage and despair as worthy subtexts for the art of song—well, golly, if we're going to be square enough to say the word *art* out loud—then it's natural to point out that American musicians have, over the past century or so, produced bountiful quantities of the most soulful art in the world. So intrinsically is American music linked to that idea of "noble warmth" that we can practically use certain names from the American canon as *synonyms* for soul: Ray Charles and James Brown, Billie Holiday and Johnny Cash, Robert Johnson and Michael Stipe, Frank Sinatra and Patsy Cline, Charlie Parker and Miles Davis and John Coltrane, Duke Ellington and the Gershwins, Howlin' Wolf and Bob Dylan, Prince and Paul Westerberg, LL Cool J and Bruce Springsteen, Captain Beefheart and Aimee Mann, Los Lobos and Lucinda Williams, Marvin Gaye and Willie Nelson, Iggy Pop and Patti Smith, Paul Simon and Tom Waits, Jeff Tweedy and Elliott Smith, Cat Power and the White Stripes.

When I was younger and I had the chance to travel around Europe, I always found that I'd start going into a kind of junkie's agony of withdrawal after a few days away from American music. Everywhere you go on the Continent, whether it's Paris or Moscow or some isolated village in Andalusia, you hear the strange, repetitive, Borat-like *zinky-zinky-zinky-zink* of European dance music. You hear it in taxis, in bars, in airports. Whether anyone actually likes this stuff, I don't know—as far as I can tell, nobody even notices that the music is *on*—but you've got to be impressed by its totalitarian-kitsch ubiquity. Why Europe continues to manufacture new permutations of the songs is a mystery to me, too, because each European dance track is indistinguishable from the next. Each one begins with a coked-up electronic rhythm track that seems to have been accelerated just a few beats too fast—if you've just gotten off a long flight, hearing this music can literally make you carsick—*zinky-zinky-zinky-zinky-zinky-zinky-zink*—and after that's gone on for a predictable number of measures, a voice, usually female, although not discernibly human, will begin skipping along like Annie Hall in the k-hole: *la-di-da-di-da, la-di-da-di-da, la-di-da-di-da, la-di-da-di-da, zinky-zinky-zinky-zinky, la-di-da-di-DA, zinky-zinky-zinky-zinky, la-di-da-di-DA* . . .

A week in Europe never fails to leave me so sick of this dance music that the slightest passing puff of American soul—Fats Waller's piano rolls pealing out of an apartment window, Cheap Trick's "Surrender" stomping away in a pub—is enough to carry me away. And yet a strange thing started happening around the beginning of the twenty-first century. I'd come back from a trip to Europe, and I'd climb into a cab at JFK, and . . . I'd hear European dance music all over again. *Here.* Only this time *Americans* were making the stuff. Nor did it stop with music. Although it's common for countries around the world to bitch about American cultural imperialism, the irony is that the feed tube has been gushing in the opposite direction for quite a while now. We are being re-made into Europe. *American Idol, Survivor, Big Brother*—all these prime-time reality shows became a phenomenon in Europe before savvy American producers decided to import them. It's hard to admit, but we're turning into Luxembourg.

Beatles for Sale: Las Vegas, 2006

Before I head for the Strip, I go to the Hard Rock for a drink. The first thing I see is the Nirvana shrine. If you walk through the main entrance of the Hard Rock Hotel & Casino—where the long white limos pull up—and step to the left, you'll see a protective pane of glass. Behind it you'll find the Nirvana memorabilia: a sleeveless flannel shirt, a six-string with the words "This Guitar Supported by the Timber Industry" scrawled iconoclastically across its hull in Magic Marker, and a massive poster of Kurt Cobain with the words "I Hate Myself and Want to Die."

I glance at this grunge reliquary for a while and then head deeper into the hotel. Pretty soon I get to the registration desk. Your average Courtyard by Marriott might be inclined to greet you with the words "Welcome to Spokane!" but here in Vegas I find a special benediction beaming out at me in a sunshiny arc: "Here We Are Now, Entertain Us."

Anyone who still nurtures the idea that there's a flourishing link between pop music and "revolution" needs to book a flight to Las Vegas. The Hard Rock doesn't make any distinction between *good* and *bad, authentic* and *cheesy.* Within spitting distance of Saint Cobain's Chapel, for instance, you'll see the shrine to Britney Spears. The Sacred Heart schoolgirl togs, the jailbait thigh-highs, the puck-heeled clogs—all the Louisiana Lolita's ". . . Baby One More Time" vestments get prime real estate right in the center of the foyer. You'll find Bruce Springsteen's noble-ballad-for-the-workin'-man memorabilia next to the entrance to Nobu, and if you wander around the floor of the casino, you'll see a blackjack table garnished with anarchy symbols.

I order a vodka and tonic. I listen to the music. The sound system in the casino is so amazing that I feel as though I'm getting the sonic equivalent of a seaweed wrap. As I sit there at the Viva Las Vegas Lounge with my cocktail, I expect to hear all the FM-radio warhorses that were long ago swallowed up by banks and beer commercials—you know, "Takin' Care of Business" and "Respect," "Behind Blue Eyes" and "Born to Be Wild." But I don't. The casino operators are smarter than that. These guys must have McKinsey & Company brain scans that allow them to Google-map the Gen-X psychographic, because what I hear coming out of their thousand-eyed spider of speakers is Radiohead's "Paranoid Android," Social Distortion's "Ball and Chain," Warren Zevon's "Lawyers, Guns and Money," Green Day's "American Idiot"—good songs, "subversive" songs, misanthropic and wry. You have to wonder what Thom Yorke, he of the dystopian vistas and the sadly gnomic bleating, would make of the line "ambition makes you look pretty ugly" firing up an army of cocktail waitresses and blackjack players.

Well, whatever—never mind. Maybe a couple of anarchy symbols aren't going to do it for you, but, eventually, just as Gen X sputters into its retirement years, the evil geniuses of the Nevada Gaming Commission will figure out a way to make you part with your hard-earned Fidelity chicken feed. You can count on that. Maybe it'll be *Bring the Noise: Jennifer Aniston Performs the Songs of Public Enemy*. Or *Miserable!*, an interpretive dance extravaganza featuring pierced contortionists from the Jim Rose Circus Sideshow and the music of the Smiths.

Wait. I'd go see that.

X

Anyway, I am here in Las Vegas to see what happened to the baby boomers.

"To withdraw, to go away, to disappear," Dennis Hopper informs me one evening when I'm watching TV. He's pacing around on a tropical beach. The Spencer Davis Group's "Gimme Some Lovin'" is pumping away in the background. Hopper is on fire. The man is ranting like the hippie shutterbug he played in *Apocalypse Now*, except that instead of talking about madness and power and divinity, he's talking about the awesome stuff the boomers can do with all the cash they've socked away. "That's how the dictionary defines retirement. Time to redefine! Your generation is definitely not headed for bingo night. In fact, you could write a book about how you're going to turn retirement upside down. 'Cause I just don't see you playing shuffleboard, you know what I mean?"

Yeah, baby. Billy from *Easy Rider* has cashed in a chunk of his radical capital by appearing in a commercial for Ameriprise, a financial services company. Ameriprise calls it the Dreams Don't Retire campaign, and it's aimed at boomers who are tarting up for their golden years. Judging from ads like this—and in 2007, they're all over the place—the boomers have every intention to *own* retirement in the same hog-at-a-trough way that they've rammed their snouts into music, food, money, exercise, and sex. "A growing number of new ventures are targeting aging baby boomers, their obsessions in the final third of their lives—and their $2 trillion in annual spending power," writes the *Wall Street Journal*. "Start-up magazines with titles like *GeezerJock, Grand* and *What's Next* are beckoning to boomers with advice on triathlons, grandchildren or new careers."

Well, unfortunately for Dennis Hopper, the boomers *do* have their own version of bingo night, and it's playing twice a night at the Mirage. What brings me to Las Vegas is not money, but love. More precisely, it's *LOVE*, the Cirque du Soleil spectacle based on the music of the Beatles. If anything is going to tell us where the wild hogs are headed, I figure it's a bunch of mimes and acrobats turning "Come Together" into a Bangkok floor show.

See, you can talk all you want about triathlons, but what's really going on with the boomers is that they've entered the phase of Total Nostalgia. On the same day I'm in Vegas, Bob Dylan, back in New York City, is testing out the waters with a Broadway musical. This is what Ben Brantley has to say about it in the *New York Times*: "Will the idealistic Coyote take up his father's whip to exploit the leadership-hungry clowns? Will he steal Cleo from Dad? Will he create a more benign world order? Hint: The show begins with Coyote looking soulfully into the audience to intone, with ominousness and dewy hope, 'The Times They Are A-Changin'.'"

Read that again if you need to.

Leadership-hungry clowns?

Let's chew on this for a moment: *Bob Dylan has a Broadway musical.* So does Abba. So does Billy Joel. John Lennon and the Beach Boys had Broadway musicals, too, although theirs mercifully faceplanted within a few days, which is exactly what's about to happen to the Bob Dylan one. You see this stuff and you can't help but imagine a lost chapter from a David Foster Wallace novel. Maybe someday they'll build Imagine, Nevada, an entire city of boomer nostalgia, a place where Botox-taut, artificial-hipped blue hairs dutifully ride the people mover from Donovan's animatronic *Mellow Yellow* magic show all the way to the Ashram, Steve Wynn's guru-themed casino complex, and then loop back around to the *Icons!* corpse-viewing center at Caesars Palace, where the embalmed bodies of Gloria Steinem and Abbie Hoffman are laid out in the style of Lenin's tomb.

I finish my drink and head for the Mirage. At the entrance, a bunch of tourists are gawking at a glassed-in tank. When I stop to see what they're looking at, it turns out to be the White Tiger Habitat, where one of Siegfried and Roy's ebony-and-ivory jungle cats is pacing back and forth in a crumbly artificial grotto.

As I putter my way into *LOVE* with the 6:45 p.m. crowd, we're escorted through the lobby by "Tomorrow Never Knows." The song still sounds amazing, with all those squealing backward-flying birdies and that thumping-waterfall drum loop. "Turn off your mind, relax and float downstream," John Lennon chants. "It is not dying, it is not dying . . . it is shining . . . it is knowing." Actually, judging from those who have joined me for the 6:45 show, it is balding, it is waddling, and it is wheezing and coughing with what sounds an awful lot like emphysema. The early birds lined up for *LOVE* are, to put it generously, an older crowd, and I find that reassuring. Everyone says that boomers are obsessed with clinging to their youth, but there's no hiding the fact that most of these Beatlemaniacs sucking on Hard Day's Night cocktails out of plastic cups have logged some heavy mileage on the long and winding road. To put it bluntly, they're old people. There's no hiding it. I watch a couple in blindingly white hospital sneakers serenading each other to "Maxwell's Silver Hammer," and I realize that all the retirement commercials in the world are not going to turn these swingers into geriatric skydivers.

Let me stress here that I have nothing against the music of the Beatles. Most of it I love. On the other hand, I don't really want to hear *about* the Beatles anymore. I've heard enough. If I somehow spend the rest of my days without ever being subjected to another rumination about why Paul McCartney is barefoot on the cover of *Abbey Road*, I will be just fine with that.

The British comedy show *Big Train* once aired a sketch called "George Martin Kidnapped." In it, Sir George, the man who produced most of the Fab Four's albums, is captured by Middle Eastern militants. But Martin finds a clever way to escape. He manages to drive the terrorists out of their gourds with boredom by prattling on and on about what it was like to work with the Beatles. His captors can't take it anymore. They're so sick of hearing about the magical mystery tour that they're forced to let him go.

That's how I feel at *LOVE*, the music directors of which, not coincidentally, are George Martin and his son Giles. There's a misty cloud of *weariness* hanging over the whole thing. Maybe it's total-nostalgia fatigue. Maybe it's because the audience has been up all night drinking and gambling or playing shuffleboard or something, but everybody I meet in the lobby seems really tired. They keep on talking about the Beatles even though they don't seem to have the energy for it. I'm not sure they can stop. *Paul was always my favorite they called him the Cute Beatle ha ha ha Oh I liked George he was the Quiet Beatle I saw them on the Ed Sullivan Show but you couldn't even hear the music there was so much screaming yep uh-huh that's why they called it Beatlemania the Beatles changed the world cough cough honey where'd you put my lozenges?* Hear enough of it and your mind starts to turn into the equivalent of North Korea, a place where saintly pictures of glorious leader Kim Jong Il are plastered on every single wall and shopwindow, and, thanks to the bountiful generosity of Kim Jong Il, you are free to spend all your leisure time pondering the true and glorious majesty of Kim Jong Il. *It is shining . . . it is shining . . .*

As we take our seats, men and women dressed up like psychedelic Buckingham Palace guards bark at us in fake British accents to let us know that photography is not permitted. Then the lights go down. A few Cirque du Soleil hobo clowns march out to rally our spirits. "Let's all help each other to make the world a better place and send out those love vibrations!" a skid-row harlequin squeals a few rows away from me. "Let's get high on love!"

LOVE turns out to be the strangest show I have ever seen. When you hear the words "Las Vegas show," you tend to think of the fat Elvis, Wayne Newton, Sammy Davis Jr.—a campy and moldy mode of entertainment, maybe, but *still fun*, right? *LOVE* is not fun. Nor is it campy—at least not in the Polynesian umbrella-drink-and-pupu-platter sense of the word. *LOVE* is a spectacle of death. If you were a kid raised in the Amazon rain forest who had never heard the Beatles, the general impression that you would get from *LOVE* is that they were some kind of creepy, *Oliver Twisty* circus act—a group of smudged Liverpool street urchins who had escaped the clutches of a scowling preacher in order to become cartwheeling Bombay mimes.

Clearly, the show wants to be some kind of a grand valedictory for the boomers. *Look what we accomplished! Before we got here, the world was gray and puritanical! After us, the world became a carnival of smiles and bright colors!* But that's not the feeling you come away with. In fact, parts of the show feel like a journey into one of those hell houses that born-again Christians put together on Halloween, only in this case the goblins and ghouls are flashing the peace sign. You have never heard "Revolution" unless you've seen it accompanied by a troop of bearded Charlie Manson impersonators leaping on trampolines.

Nor have you ever really *understood* "Drive My Car" until you've seen a team of howling acrobats rolling a Volkswagen Beetle onto a stage in the middle of the chorus.

Nor have you ever really listened to "Blackbird"—yes, "Blackbird"—unless you've heard it sung by a German proctologist.

I don't want to get all high and mighty about this, but what the Cirque du Soleil people do to "Blackbird" ought to get them dragged into a courtroom in The Hague. It is a desecration. It is a violation of all that is holy and natural. I can't believe my ears. First, the song stops—the delicate lilt of Paul McCartney's melody simply cuts out. Then some mad-professor guy dressed up in a white lab coat starts yapping out the lyrics in a harsh Mitteleuropean accent that suggests a cross between Marilyn Manson in his Weimar-cabaret phase and the gestapo on *Hogan's Heroes*. "Blackbud zinging in za DEAD of NIIIGHT! TAKE dese SUNKEN eyes und LEARN to ZEE!" Now and then he breaks into a cackle. There are four acrobats dressed up as blackbirds. When the doctor yells at them, the birds start to flap and caw hysterically. *CAW-CAW-CAW-CAW!*

Have I misread the program?

Are they . . . crows?

What the hell is going on?

Just at the moment when I think, *This cannot get any worse*, Dr. Gestapo slips on a blue rubber grove, leers at the crowd, and mimes the act of shoving a gloved finger up a blackbird's rectum.

INTERMISSION:
TO HELL WITH POVERTY
2006

POOR BUOYANCY: The realization that one was a better person when one had less money.

—*Douglas Coupland*, Generation X

Historically speaking, slackers and yuppies have been portrayed as archenemies, which is ironic, if you think about it, because many of them were after the same thing: the maximization of leisure. Yuppies wanted to attain it by working gruesome hours. Slackers wanted to attain it by not working at all. There's not necessarily a *gaping* chasm between a person who's persnickety about Guided By Voices B sides and a person who's persnickety about the various grades of imported *toro*.

On the other hand, most Xers are aware, if only subliminally, that the rise of the original yuppies in the early eighties coincided with the exact point at which the boomers decided to throw in the towel on saving the world and began, instead, doing lucrative consulting work for Union Carbide. "Much of the energy and optimism and passion of the '60s seems to have been turned inward, on lives, careers, apartments and dinners," *Newsweek* noted in its "Year of the Yuppie" cover story at the end of 1984—the same year, not coincidentally, that the Replacements released *Let It Be*.

Yuppies frequently describe a kind of epiphany, a sudden realization that poverty might never live up to its romantic promise. To Amy Caplan, 30, the Eastern sales manager for CBS Radio, it came just weeks after she embarked on her long-standing dream of being a social worker, and found herself in the cheerless confines of a state home for severely retarded elderly men. She also got her first paycheck. "I realized that I would have to make a commitment to being poor to be a social worker," she says. "Eventually, I was able to shed the notion that to prove to everybody I was a good person I had to parade around as a good person by being a social worker."

It's fascinating to read *Newsweek*'s "Year of the Yuppie" story now, because a huge portion of it happens to be about food. That "epiphany" that lured so many boomers away from a life of toil and sacrifice? Well, it all began with a nibble of cheese. "How many lives," the magazine breathlessly mused, "have been shaped by that first taste of Brie?"

A used copy of *The Yuppie Handbook* recently fell into my hands. The book was published in paperback in 1984 as a jokey jag of social anthropology, and it made a slew of observations about this new American species. The yuppie's lifestyle preferences were apparently viewed as so bizarre that they were bound to elicit populist chuckles and guffaws. Here are some of the things, according to *The Yuppie Handbook*, that the budding yupster could not live without: gourmet coffee, running shoes, a Cuisinart, a renovated kitchen with a double sink, the smoked mozzarella from Dean & DeLuca, a housekeeper, a mortgage, a Coach bag, a Gucci briefcase, and a Rolex. *Oh, har har har, that crazy yup!* The yuppie could be found listening to Bessie Smith and Bob Marley and the Police on a tiny device attached to headphones, working off stress with shiatsu massage and a facial, learning as much as possible about fine wine, traveling around the world on vacation, working out in a health club, drinking bottled water, typing away at a computer while sitting in an ergonomic chair, and (the clincher) eating tuna sashimi for lunch. The mere mention of tuna sashimi for lunch was apparently seen as the height of hilarity back in 1984. "A yuppie most nearly approaches sainthood," said the book, "when he or she is able to accomplish more things in a single day than is humanly possible." This was *before* cell phones and BlackBerries.

All of which means that the archetypal yuppie of the eighties sounds, to an ominous degree, like *everyone you know*. Well, maybe not everyone, but close. What we have these days is a diverse spectrum of yuppiness: guppies, buppies, indie yups, paleo-yups, luxe yups, schlub yups, dharma yups, tyro yups, crypto-yups. Former edge-dwelling slackers might be discreet enough to make their conspicuous consumption appear sort of casual and offhand—and therefore inconspicuous—but that doesn't mean they're consuming any less of the sumptuous enticements they used to spurn. (Don't kid yourself, the people creating a boom market for organic baby food and Niman Ranch bacon are not subsistence-level hippies.) Officially speaking, the yuppie was thought to have died on October 19, 1987, when that day's stock market crash, and a subsequent recession, ushered in the underdog sensibility that held tenacious sway in the American headspace until 1994 or so, but by now an argument could be made that the yuppie phenomenon is the most enduring and influential social movement of the past fifty years.

I've occasionally thought that the chamber in the American household that has done the most to mold the Gen-X sensibility—*after* the room where your parents put the TV in the seventies, I mean—is the grotty apartment bathroom. For years I attended to my daily grooming in bathrooms that were only a couple of notches better than the one Ewan McGregor dove into at the beginning of *Trainspotting*. Whenever I rented an apartment—in Prague, in Santa Barbara, in New York City—I went through a process of acceptance during which I had to learn once again to make friends with rust and mildew, with Saturn-like rings of discoloration in the toilet, with ejaculations of silt and yellowish foam whenever I turned on the faucet. If you want to talk about "Year of the Yuppie" epiphanies, well, a wedge of Brie has got nothing on a showerhead that coughs a little jellyfish of sewage onto your head when you're getting ready for a job interview.

Not long ago, for the first time in our lives, my wife and I burned through a wad of money and renovated a bathroom. I didn't expect to care. But then, our new temple of cleansing and excreting was done, and I stood underneath a hot and steady jet of clean water, surrounded by a Gatsbyish mosaic of black-and-white subway tiles, and stepped out to shave at one of those bosomy white sinks that you encounter in four-star hotels. . . .

Now I cared.

"When you're twenty-seven or twenty-eight, your body starts emitting the Sheraton enzyme," Douglas Coupland told *People* in 1991. "You can no longer sleep on people's floors."

By thirty-seven, the Sheraton enzyme has more often than not mutated into the Four Seasons endorphin. People, like neighborhoods, have a tendency to gentrify. On a trip to the West Coast, I go back to the old precinct of Pasadena that used to be my beloved slacker drag strip when I was in high school in the eighties—a scroungy wonderland of pawn shops, espresso bars, dive pubs, taco trucks, racks full of vintage clothes, and shelves full of used books. As I drive around, it comes as a minor shock to see that every single trace of that suburban bohoscape is now gone, replaced by upscale trattorias and tapas bars, Crate & Barrel and Pottery Barn and Tiffany. While the yuppies were colonizing my favorite neighborhood, apparently they were doing the same thing to my brain.

3. I WILL DARE
2006–PRESENT: NOT SUCKING

Really, what's to gain from saying that the night only grows darker and that hope lies crushed under the jackboots of the wicked?

> —*Farewell essay from the final issue of* Might *magazine, July/August 1997*

We gon' get it together, right?
I believe that.

> —*Mos Def, "Fear Not of Man"*

Minute by minute we move toward the restoration.

> —*Joshua Beckman, "Let the People Die"*

The Poetry Bus Saves the World

Okay, so everybody on the bus knows Montana is going to be good—maybe even intense, possibly flat-out momentous—but we've got no idea how right we are until the Green Tortoise starts to inch down a curled-rattlesnake driveway into the Butler Creek Ranch. The ranch lies on twenty-three Edenic acres a few miles outside of Missoula. It looks like a bowl—there's a house and a field ringed all around by piney slopes. People at the bottom of the bowl are grinning and jumping and waving at us, which is really nice. After a long and groggy drive from Spokane, we, the ten passengers on the Poetry Bus, are prepared to get stoked: *Hey, look down there! Yes! O wonderful waving and grinning and jumping people of Montana! You're freakin' hungry for it, aren't you?! Hungry for . . . poetry! Yes! Watch how we descend from the peaks of the Bitterroot Range like conquering warriors!*

Except something's off. Something isn't right.

We get the news as soon as we lumber out of the Green Tortoise: *chaos.* Just a few minutes before our heroic entrance, an aficionado of verse apparently went kind of bonkers. People at the ranch were watching the guy from a distance as he danced around in a black suit and a bowler hat and took swigs from a bottle of something that was most likely not Mountain Dew. Then all of a sudden the cowboy droog had hopped into his mammoth white SUV, backed it straight through the ranch's fence, uprooted some posts, peeled off toward the porta-potty as if this were the Annual Arthur Rimbaud Monster Truck Rally, and burned rubber down a dirt path into the brush. There, he'd collided with a tree, flipped his gas guzzler, crawled out of the wreckage, and bolted up a hill on foot.

But he's all right, the locals assure us. In fact, he's out there running around in the woods. But hey, welcome to Montana!

So the crowd is *still processing* all this when the Poetry Bus arrives, because of course one does not generally attend a poetry reading expecting to see an outtake from *The Dukes of Hazzard.* "This is very rock and roll, I have to say," a bespectacled MFA student muses as cop cars, fire engines, ambulances, and tow trucks begin snaking down into the bowl and heading over to the crash site. Giving American poetry a rock-and-roll transfusion—well, you might say that's one of the explicit goals of the Poetry Bus. And yet this particular style of merry prank—a one-man demolition derby—well, that's not at all what Joshua Beckman and Matthew Zapruder had in mind when they dreamed up the transcontinental tour.

After we wait around for a tense couple of hours, our friends in law enforcement determine that the Poetry Bus and all these word-hungry westerners are welcome to stick around, just as long as they don't smoke cigarettes near the dry grass in the middle of the fire season. "We're on!" says poet Anthony McCann, pumping his fist. In spite of, or maybe because of, the bizarre saga of the demon SUV, the Wednesday-night reading at the Butler Creek Ranch winds up feeling like something for the history books: one of those rare moments of we're-all-on-the-same-wavelength connection. The night is cool, the air is fragrant with forest-fire ash, the audience is prone to cheering and hooting, the podium's a stack of logs, and the sound system is so fiber-optically loud and clear that you can hear the way the readers breathe in between each line and the sound of every poem booming away in the hills. Erin Belieu, Katy Lederer, Melanie Noel, Catherine Wing, McCann, Zapruder, Beckman—all these poets in their thirties are like members of a nomadic indie band that's been wandering around the sagebrush for years, living on locusts and honey and looking for their tribe, and they've finally found it.

McCann, his dark hair flopping to and fro and his jeans in a perpetual state of ass-crack free fall, hits the dais like the life of the party, bobbing and weaving. His timing is so fluidly spot-on that he leaves the audience both awed and in stitches.

Katy Lederer's inflections are sharp, nuanced, pulsating; she treats each poem with the sort of meticulous care that a spider might bring to the task of devouring a trapped fly.

Erin Belieu gives a ferocious reading of a single poem from *Black Box*, called "Pity." ("Once I took it in my mouth, I had to / admit, pity tastes good, like the sandwiches / they make in French patisseries, the loaf smeared / with force-fed organs, crust that shreds the skin behind / your teeth.") Then she tells the crowd that altitude sickness has made her too woozy to go on. Which, of course, feels *perfect*.

X

For three days in September of 2006 I was embedded on the Wave Books Poetry Bus as it traveled from Seattle to Spokane to Missoula—the first leg of a trip that would eventually wobble its way through Lincoln and Omaha, Minneapolis and Pittsburgh, Boston and Austin, Las Vegas and Santa Fe, New York and New Orleans. From the Gen-X standpoint, it might be useful to think of Wave Books as the Sub Pop of American poetry: based in Seattle, owned and underwritten by the wealthy arts patron Charlie Wright, and edited in a partnership between Joshua Beckman and Matthew Zapruder, Wave is an independent publishing house that's all about newness and risk and West Coast brio. The Poetry Bus tour would give those principles a road test.

I wanted to tag along because I happen to believe there's a renaissance under way in American poetry—a movement, brimming over with Gen Xers, that the mass-media matrix remains too navel-gazing and Paris Hilton fixated to recognize. And yeah, I wanted to tag along because I figured that lurching around the country in a bus full of poets sounded like a gas, in a Putumayo/ biodiesel sort of way. You hear about a great American road trip such as this one and you can't help but think: *On the Road*, *The Electric Kool-Aid Acid Test*, *Fear and Loathing in Las Vegas*, Lewis and Clark. A squadron of like-minded and free-spirited people getting sloppy wasted and heading out on the highway for a thirteen-thousand-mile marathon from Stagnation to Bliss.

But I had an anthropological interest, too. I wanted to spend time with a few of the most marginalized Gen Xers I could find, and, aside from convicted criminals, I couldn't think of anyone more marginalized than a poet. In the United States at the beginning of

the twenty-first century, poets were like the humanoids seques-
tered in that bunker in *Beneath the Planet of the Apes*. They toiled in
darkness while the simian world thumped its chest above.

And yet: Here they were, climbing aboard a bus together. Here
they were, setting out to visit fifty cities in fifty days. Here they
were, in the face of yawning indifference, trying to awaken something of the soulful weirdness that they'd always loved about America. Here they were, injecting the X back into the national bloodstream. It's not as though the poets were unaware of their obscurity.
It's simply that they had decided to do something about it. These
American anchorites would not go gentle into a good night of apes
and athazagoraphobia. One way or another they were going to
inflict themselves on America, eating up thirteen thousand miles
in a vehicle emblazoned with big ridiculous red letters on the side:
POETRY BUS. They would blog from the bus, shoot digital-video
footage on the bus, send out podcasts from the bus. They would
recite their poetry in sushi bars if they had to.

I got to Seattle on a Sunday morning, two days before the bus
began its eastward chug. I was scheduled to meet Joshua Beckman,
known as one of the best young poets in America and a genuine
force at the podium. Beckman's readings could swing back and
forth between radiance and petulance, lethargy and liturgy. Passages
such as this one left audiences transfixed:

> *and I saw the best minds of my generation*
> *living in lofts*
> *thinking they were the best minds of their generation*
> *while the world hacked up tax breaks and jet fighters*

Beckman picked me up in an aging Honda that was cluttered with
used books. Together we traveled back in time—to 1991, or maybe
it was 1816, I'm not sure. The Honda ferried us to Beckman's
apartment. He lived in Seattle's Capitol Hill neighborhood, in a spa-
cious flat for which he paid $1,000 a month. He had no television,

but he did have a couple of turntables, and of course he had vinyl. *Boxes* of vinyl, and the best kind: obscure, heavy, scratched up, the covers yellowed. Relics, these records were—shards from the ruins of the lost civilization of X. Beckman's crates bulged with tabla music from Rajasthan, jazz nocturnes from Stork-Clubby Gotham watering holes, shouts and spirituals from the islands off the coast of South Carolina, a musty reading by Wallace Stevens, pop stomps by the Dave Clark Five, prim marches by John Philip Sousa. His bookshelves, too, enshrined modes of thinking that had spin-drifted so far out of the glare that they almost qualified as Papua New Guinean. Beckman had a very soft spot for the Romantics, and his library was dominated by the works of Percy Bysshe Shelley, Samuel Taylor Coleridge, and William Wordsworth, along with arcane tracts exploring the link between the imagination and opium. His place reminded me of the underground chamber where V, the masked and suave antihero of *V for Vendetta*, sequesters himself after England succumbs to a fascist lockdown: a cool, hidden cellar lined with old books, sound-tracked by a jukebox

If the X agent could be cultivated in a laboratory, the petri dish might look a lot like Joshua Beckman's apartment. On one hand, here he sat in the city of Microsoft and Amazon.com. Seattle palpably pulsed with technology—for all we knew, those fog banks coming off Puget Sound were laced with nanobots. At the same time, Beckman remained drawn to old things, to relics living on in a state of radiant obsolescence. His obsessions were tactile, preelectronic, offhand, off-line, off the grid. He talked about typewriters—how he would scour dusty shops in Seattle looking for secretarial-pool models that had been phased out decades ago. He gave me a couple of chapbooks that he'd been printing up and distributing on his own, by hand. One of them was made up of journal entries that he had composed over the course of four days in February. He had peppered it with quotations from his favorite writers—all those Romantic poets and thinkers. I opened the flap and found this: "No copyright. Reproduce at will." And then this:

Daily, it seems, we are being called to task by the country we live in ... We have gathered our talents and our knowledge with the sense that they are the useful tools to make our way in the world and have found them far more than undervalued, we have found them embraced for the qualities that keep them neutralized ... Even to say *we* is an enormous leap of its own, but over and over a sense appears that not only is there a "we" but that it is the very notion that we build our optimism on.

Right now I am confused. I am confused by my own sense of urgent necessity, and my inability to meet it with action even slightly equal to its scope. I am confused by the role that I, as a poet, must take. And I am confused that I can learn more about what is going on around me from a pile of two-hundred-year-old books than from the *New York Times*.

There is little in trying that doesn't seem foolish. Every attempt is awkward and every revolution somehow silly.

Beckman had spent a few years living on the fringe—for a while he'd been almost penniless in Staten Island, subsisting on brief spurts of income from odd jobs—but in these chapbooks it was clear that he was giving voice to feelings that even the more yuppified corporate soldiers of our generation were grappling with. And ironically, Beckman was about to give his "own sense of urgent necessity" a kick in the pants.

Although they were planning to get on a bus and travel all over the country reading poetry, Beckman and Zapruder had no utopian illusions. They didn't talk about a "revolution" springing up in their wake. Such talk, in fact, made them wince. And even though the two of them had P. T. Barnumishly hyped up the bus tour as "the biggest literary event of 2006," they weren't dreamers, and their goal, albeit commendable, remained very simple: they just wanted to introduce more people to some great poetry that the mass media chose to ignore.

Poetry readings—in the age of Gawker and TMZ and *American Idol*? What could possibly be more earnest, more Maynard G. Krebs, more *undergraduate*? Were poetry readings still legal under the PATRIOT Act? Would bongo drums be involved? The scheme ran so flagrantly counter to the prevailing national business model that you could only stand back and gape in admiration. "In spite of the proliferation of media right now, people feel lost," Beckman told me that evening in his apartment, as he tried to explain the enterprise. "They don't know where to go for dialogue. There's a desire for communication." You could tell he was hesitant to talk about it—he didn't want to see the whole thing misinterpreted, reduced to yet another "quirky" insurgency. He got out some rolling papers and a packet of Drum and fixed himself a cigarette. He lit it. Inhaled. Savored the smoke. Exhaled. And landed upon the simplest explanation he could find.

"A desire to be heard," he said.

X

"Spokane is kicking ass, though," Matthew Zapruder said. "You *go*, Spokane. You *go*, midsize city in the midday sun. *Thank* you for passing that law against insomnia, Spokane."

The Poetry Bus had reached the end of its first day of travel. We were rolling past burger joints and flophouses, nail salons and thrift stores. A marquee outside one of the pawnshops was lit up with something that, in its succinct way, qualified as an American poem:

> *Surly Staff.*
> *Poor Selection.*
> *High Prices.*
> *Terrible Quality.*

"This," Zapruder said of Spokane, "is where you go after your fourth divorce."

Zapruder, who happened to be the grandson of Abraham Zapruder, the Dallas businessman who'd caught footage of the Kennedy assassination on his Bell & Howell Zoomatic camera, proved to be a master of the scalding wisecrack. On the bus he and Beckman were like Han Solo and Chewbacca in the cockpit of the *Millennium Falcon*. Zapruder supplied the comic patter; Beckman would respond with a chesty rumble. I admired these two gentleman-insurgents for having the balls to put this logistical nightmare together, but I admired them even more when we started moving that day and I realized that these two old friends were facing a new wrinkle in Murphy's Law every time they turned around. We weren't even out of Seattle's suburban gridlock when Beckman realized that one of the bus windows refused to close. He held it in place with his hands until we pulled in to a rest stop. Somewhere in the middle of Washington, poet Melanie Noel lay sleeping at the back of the bus when the Green Tortoise began farting and growling and she was blanketed by a freakish wind of carbon monoxide and heat. A panel inside the bus, right above the rear tires, had somehow shimmied loose and popped open, exposing everyone to baking exhaust fumes. Beckman raced back and clamped the panel shut with his own size-sixteen feet. We pulled in to another rest stop. Along the way people would ask the two of them, "What's the *point*? What's the Poetry Bus *about*?" After traveling with them on the Green Tortoise, I came to feel that this shotgun tango between bedlam and bliss *was* the point, that what we were witnessing was a tragically obscure and insular American art form getting reacquainted with the stresses and obstacles of the real world. Which could only be good for the art form. If the most common beef against much of American poetry is that it's cut off from American life, well, I couldn't think of a better remedy than to ride out on a forty-foot bus and take poetry straight into a pandemonium of Wal-Mart and *American*

Idol and killer gas prices and gastric bypass surgery and Grand Theft Auto.

The point was to promote poetry, right, but also to promote something else—a mind-set, the very possibility of considering poetry as an antidote to the monotony of the matrix. "If I'd been a kid at a rest stop and I'd seen these people pouring out of a poetry bus, I never would have forgotten that for the rest of my life," Zapruder told me. "I believe in changing the context for poetry. I can't stand the way people think of poetry. Poetry is a process of being awakened to the thing you're being awakened to, and it's the same thing with this bus. We don't *know* what'll fuckin' happen."

YouTube Saves the World

> Like any good virus, Gen X also produces mutations.
>
> —*Douglas Coupland, in* Details, *March 2002*

That observation of Zapruder's—"We don't know what'll fuckin' happen"—contains more force than you might expect.

We have entered the age of *we don't know what'll fuckin' happen*, and that is a positive development. And we have reached that development *because* of Gen Xers—because of their enterprise, and because of their willingness to do an end run around the dominant modes of communication. What's both inspiring and disorienting about this brave new world is that Xers invented the template for it.

Before there were blogs, there were zines. A zine was a personal and idiosyncratic alternative to established newspapers and magazines, but since the editor of a zine was saddled with cumbersome methods of manufacturing and distribution—paper, staples, ink cartridges, the U.S. postal system, tolerant clerks willing to put the zine in the stacks at the local book- or record store—her audience was limited. She could only mail off the zine to so many Mission of Burma fans before she went broke or was driven mad by the tedium.

A blog is a zine liberated from the annoyances of physical form. Because of that, it can—when lightning strikes—reach tens of millions of people in a single day. The same could be said about the new world of webcam storytelling. Before there was YouTube, there was public-access cable. If you had a video camera and gobs of time on your hands and you were friendly with some dude down at the station, you could—à la Wayne and Garth—record your bong-hit bons mots in the basement and air them at four in the morning on channel 73. Now, thanks to video-sharing sites such as YouTube, anyone can post a skit or a treatise—*right now,* with a click—and send it out into an invisible landscape populated by millions. That clip could, hypothetically, change the world. Better yet—especially for Xers who like to fret about how all the fun things are gobbled up by the mainstream—that clip could change a *portion* of the world while the rest of the world knows nothing about it. Which is what we always wanted, isn't it?

Few things are more cherished by Xers than the idea of an indie record company—a label (like Sub Pop and Twin / Tone and Matador) that is freed from the shackles of the corporate cheese merchants, that doesn't have to dumb down in a crass grab for colossal profits. Indies have released some of the most stirring and original records of the past twenty years, but to romanticize the "freedom" of an indie label is to savor a sugar-coated delusion. Indies are always short on cash—why do you think they wind up partnering with the same conglom overlords they're supposed to despise?—and now that radio stations seethe with antagonism toward anything new or strange, indies have to fight like cornered badgers to get anyone to pay attention. Suddenly, though, a band has numberless new ways to get the word out: MySpace pages, podcasts, file-sharing outposts, tastemaking troughs like Pitchfork and Stereogum and Idolator, the natural-selection process of YouTube.

Xers brought this about, and Xers benefit from it.

After traveling to Montana with the Poetry Bus, I went to YouTube and typed in "Poetry Bus." It surfaced immediately: shaky footage of Joshua Beckman at the back of the bus, his frizzed nimbus of hair swept back in a bandanna, holding a megaphone and reading a poem by Frank O'Hara. "Lana Turner has collapsed!" he proclaimed in the clip. I remembered the moment well, because it had happened at the precise instant when the bus was passing through the town of Wallace, Idaho—Lana Turner's birthplace. Before long, video clips from the Poetry Bus were bobbing around on YouTube like iambic buoys. When I caught up with the bus a month later at the Dia museum in Beacon, New York, I felt as though I'd been riding with Beckman and Zapruder the whole way.

X

That fall there came a different kind of Cooler King moment: Google bought YouTube for $1.2 billion. One's first response, of course, tended toward a kind of flabbergasted envy, but YouTube's Chad Hurley and Steve Chen had stumbled upon one of those ideas so beautiful in its simplicity—*put random video stuff on the Web*—and had executed it so joyfully that you couldn't hate them. They shot a video for their own site, a slackerish thank-you to their "community" in which they managed to come across as the stars of *Excellent Adventure 3: Bill & Ted Get Filthy Rich*. (Look, that red-and-white-striped awning—had they really decided to celebrate their good fortune at T.G.I. Friday's? *Hey, dude, I just scored hundreds of millions of dollars. Let's go get a taco salad!*) For anyone who had chosen a more traditional career route, or anyone who had secretly gloated when the dot-com meltdown of 2000 made the Silicon Valley bum-rush look like a charade, well, *this*—this came as a corrective. Not only was technology not going away—*duh*—but the big-impact innovations were just getting revved up. Here in the business pages blared the final honk of proof, if you needed any, that American media was going through a tidal shift.

Even if you considered yourself an early adopter, the YouTube/ Google deal's combination of enormity and velocity had to boggle your mind. Chen and Hurley had hatched this idea only a year before. After launching the site, they'd waited for what seemed like three or four minutes before millions of camcorder auteurs started rushing in with a canyon full of new content. The tipping point came right around Christmas of 2005, and it arrived in the form of "Lazy Sunday," a video that the boomer grandee Lorne Michaels had hesitated to air on his show, *Saturday Night Live*, probably because he was afraid that it would spook advertisers and make viewers laugh too hard. "Lazy Sunday," like those outer-space repasts that people ate on *The Jetsons*, managed to compress an entire garden's worth of Gen-X nutrients into a capsule. In the video, two white guys from opposite ends of the Gen-X spectrum, twenty-eight-year-old Andy Samberg and forty-year-old Chris Parnell, rapped themselves into a state of sawed-off fury over the details of a downtown slack. They rapped about cupcakes from the Magnolia Bakery and the magic of Google Maps, they rapped about the irresistible charms of *The Chronicles of Narnia* and the crazy deliciousness of sucking up Mr. Pibb through a Red Vine.

Nobody cared when "Lazy Sunday" showed up on *SNL*, but when the clip materialized on YouTube, offices were seized by such an epidemic of procrastination that it threatened to smother productivity and flatten the NASDAQ. Within days, "Lazy Sunday" had gotten 5 million hits. Within weeks Hurley was touching down at the annual media-mogul hoedown in Sun Valley, Idaho, where executives like Les Moonves of CBS and Phil Knight of Nike courted him as if he were a sorority sister in a miniskirt. It's hard to know whether the old guard was tempted or terrified. What YouTube was up to, after all, was nothing less than dismantling the most powerful corporate tool in American life: TV. It's not just that more and more people were watching three-minute clips instead of snoozy thirty-minute sitcoms. More and more people were making the shows on their own. As journalist and

VH1 executive Michael Hirschorn would write in the *Atlantic Monthly* a few months later:

> You don't have to be a futurehead to see that the sitcom era, and traditional television with it, is today being bookended. Video is now startlingly easy to produce, edit, and distribute. If you've watched the Web-based video-sharing site YouTube grow over the past six to eight months from Web backwater to the world's largest video outlet, you've seen Americans embrace the idea of becoming television producers and even building their own mini-networks.

Even though it was now owned by one of the world's biggest corporations, YouTube somehow seemed to stay indie to the core. In fact it was *beyond* indie, like so many Web phenomena. Anyone could post. The muse could crop up anywhere. Credentials were moot. Want to tell a story? Your MFA from the Iowa Writers' Workshop wasn't going to help you on YouTube any more than a feather would have protected you from the lions in the Colosseum. This was democratic capitalism in its most saber-toothed extreme. Tens of millions of videos sat stockpiled in servers, and only the strongest—the funniest, the most profound, the smartest, the stupidest—would survive the pruning process.

You could see it as a threat, or you could see it as an opportunity. Had Rimbaud been drunk and alive at the dawn of the twenty-first century, we probably would have found him reciting his poems into a webcam and posting them on YouTube. Blurry but oddly soulful footage of kids playing on a beach at sunset could click its way around the globe and become a twenty-first-century sacrament. A squadron of skate punks in San Luis Obispo could create the next "Smells Like Teen Spirit" video with a digital camera and a broken microphone in their parents' kitchen. The messier, the better. "In fact," wrote Hirschorn, "this grittiness, lack of polish, and occasionally shocking intimacy constitute a new aesthetic of realness, much as the scratchiness, feedback, and ostentatious amateurishness of the Sex Pistols made everything else seem like mere affectation."

X

I don't like hypnotics, you see. I mean, I'm doing a non-hypnotic music to break up the catatonic state. And I think there is one right now.

—*Experimental rock bandleader Captain Beefheart, in an old interview with Tom Snyder, unearthed on YouTube*

Gen Xers tend to cherish old things, and I know plenty of fellow butterfly collectors who remain freaked out by the overnight dominance of new things like YouTube.

But the irony is that YouTube represents the Gen-X vision in epic form. YouTube is a grand electronic version of Joshua Beckman's apartment. It consists of an endless list, a teeming database, a monastic arsenal, a curated chaos, a thrift store, a record shop— the kind of digital time capsule that the medieval monks of Ireland might have put together if they'd grown up on Dungeons & Dragons and the *Buzz Bin*. Social critics like to slag on YouTube and MySpace for being vehicles for millennial narcissism—post a video, get famous. But YouTube and MySpace, both of which were created and launched by Xers, are much more than mouse-click soapboxes. They're libraries. They're museums. They're catalogs of Cooler King moments.

Just as with Wikipedia and Gawker and Pitchfork, any random click on YouTube will whisk you down another rabbit hole. A stray impulse compels you to type the name "Beefheart" into one of those blank spaces, and, *abracadabra*, within five seconds you're watching a clip, a mind-bending clip, of Captain Beefheart, the demented and reclusive gremlin of Dada-expressionist blues—*a guy who gets no mainstream airplay ever*—ripping through "I'm Gonna Booglarise You Baby" on some German TV show in 1972. Watch that, marvel, move on. Now there's a longer clip of Beefheart being interviewed by David Letterman, along with some footage of the Captain and his Magic Band snorting and snarling through "Hot Head" on *Saturday Night Live*. No! Yes! Really? Did this happen? Dig deeper and you'll discover a six-minute Beefheart documentary put together by the equally deranged Tom Snyder. Snyder asks Beefheart about his formal education, which supposedly added up to a single day of kindergarten, and the Captain says, "If you wanna be a different fish, you've gotta jump out of the school."

Of course, not long after Google bought YouTube, corporations such as Viacom swept in to rid the site of all sorts of copyrighted material that had been stolen, they argued, from their own programs. Such an action was inevitable, but it hasn't soured the joy of the YouTube experience, at least not yet. At its best YouTube reminds us of the same article of faith that the Poetry Bus was trying to rekindle: *America is a weird place*. Writing in the December 2006 issue of *Wired*, Bob Garfield captured the charge of elation that shoots through you whenever YouTube gives you another glimpse of our republic at its most unfiltered:

> Search around some more. Type in "evolution of dance," which has got nearly 35 million views in six months. You wouldn't think "Ohio motivational speaker's grand finale" would equal "mesmerizing," but Judson Laipply's seamless sampling of footwork to 30 songs, from Elvis to 'N Sync, pretty much is. Or try the accurately titled "Noah takes a photo of himself every day for six years." A time-lapse documentary of Noah Kalina over 2,356 days, it's a little thin on plot, but it nonetheless racked up more than 3 million views in six weeks. You'd better also see "Numa Numa," which stars a chubby young

man in his New Jersey bedroom lip-synching to an insipid
but weirdly fetching Romanian pop song.

This reawakening of euphoric weirdness is no small thing.
Because just as YouTube is surging, the weirdness that you can find
on corporate TV is a very different kind from what you encounter
on YouTube. Mainstream weirdness is weirdness you're supposed
to snicker at—weirdness that makes you avert your eyes. A perfect
example is *American Idol*. Every season of *American Idol* begins with
the culling of the fold. The producers hold mass auditions across
the country, and freaks of every stripe—naked guitar-strumming
cowboys, morbidly obese castrati, wailing schizophrenics dressed
up like Wonder Woman—amble up to a platform to be gutted on
camera. It all seems rigged, of course. The freaks never stand a
chance, so this annual rite of passage has no purpose other than the
mockery of those who don't fit in.

Of course, those who don't fit in have given us some of the
greatest music in the national songbook—off the top of my
head I'm thinking of Johnny Cash, Billie Holiday, Bob Dylan, Phil
Spector, the Ramones, John Doe and Exene Cervenka, Nile Rodg-
ers, Patti Smith, Lauryn Hill, Elliott Smith, Kurt Cobain, Alejandro
Escovedo, Marvin Gaye, Lucinda Williams, Jimi Hendrix, Steely
Dan, Guided By Voices, the White Stripes—but on *American Idol*
any one of these visionary malcontents with their wobbly vocal
cords and their moody dispositions would have been trotted out to
the firing squad. On *American Idol* the "good" musicians—the ones
who, it is implied, have a future in the business—are the compliant
ones, the ones who sing purty and dress normal and say "please"
and "thank you" and "yes sir" when Simon hurls battery acid in
their face.

This is why YouTube is saving the world. Because unless some
stock-optioned overlord has already shut it down by the time this
book comes out, you can go to YouTube right now, type in "Public Enemy," and watch a seven-minute "Fight the Power" video

directed by Spike Lee, a strangely moving piece of pop-cultural debris in which Chuck D and Flavor Flav—yes, *that* Flavor Flav—lead
a massive march of brothers and sisters down a New York City
street. On YouTube you will find a shirtless Iggy Pop humping and
writhing his way through "Funtime" on a sleepy afternoon talk
show hosted by Dinah Shore. You'll find lost concert footage of
the Feelies and Hüsker Dü and the Bad Brains—preserved and
passed along to the next generation like crumbly parchment scrip-
tures. You'll find a choir of senior citizens performing Sonic Youth's
"Schizophrenia," and you'll realize that all these outcast voices
have been waiting for us all along, milling around outside the walls
of the castle.

In fact, at the same time that mass media is bombarding us with the
tabloid monotony of the star system—*Britney Britney Britney Britney*—
students of American business know that the star system is collaps-
ing. All sorts of enterprises that have been founded on Xish curatorial
principles—companies like Amazon.com and Netflix—have discovered that a substantial chunk of their sales comes from the margins.
Britney Spears is only a star when your brain stays plugged in to the
matrix; yank out the wires and another realm takes shape. Chris
Anderson, the editor of *Wired*, puts it this way in his brilliant book *The
Long Tail*:

> There's still demand for big cultural buckets, but they're
> no longer the only market. The hits now compete with
> an infinite number of niche markets, of any size. And
> consumers are increasingly favoring the one with the
> most choice. The era of one-size-fits-all is ending, and in
> its place is something new, a market of multitudes. . . .
>
> This shattering of the mainstream into a zillion differ-
> ent cultural shards is something that upsets traditional
> media and entertainment no end. After decades of exec-
> utives refining their skill in creating, picking, and pro-
> moting hits, those hits are suddenly not enough. The

audience is shifting to something else, a muddy and in-
distinct proliferation of . . . Well, we don't have a good
term for such non-hits. They're certainly not "misses,"
because most weren't aimed at world domination in the
first place. They're "everything else."

One possible name for everything else: X. You wouldn't know
it from watching *American Idol* or taking a spin through yet another
neighborhood overthrown by Applebee's, but the Gen-X stomping grounds of the past—the espresso bar, the record shop, the
thrift store—have been resurrected in digital form. The new bohemia is less a place than it is a headspace. It's flexible enough to
bypass all the old binaries. It encompasses mass *and* class, mainstream *and* marginal, yuppie *and* refusenik, gearhead *and* Luddite.
It's everywhere and it's nowhere in particular. You might shake
hands with it when the Poetry Bus rolls into your town, or you
might swim around in it the next time you log on to YouTube. It's
wide open. When you pay it a visit, you don't know what'll fuckin'
happen.

X

Tourist Experiences City by Buying Used CDs

CHARLESTON, SC—Tourist Alex Pratt decided to "get the
feel" of the historic South Carolina port city of Charleston by
making the rounds of its local used-CD stores Tuesday. "I found
a Marshall Crenshaw CD I didn't have, and really lucked out on
the Feelies' *The Good Earth*—I haven't seen that in years," said
Pratt, who has also shopped for music in Boston, San Francisco,
Gettysburg, PA, and Kansas City. "I like this place. It's a lot like
my regular used-CD shop back in Chicago."

—*From the* Onion, *October 4, 2006*

I have a middle-aged soul. When I turned 38, I said to my wife, "Am I not 40 yet?" I feel like I've been 40 for about seven years.

—*Actor Paul Giamatti, in* Parade, *July 9, 2006*

In spite of our first wave of enterprise and creativity, Generation X is still defined more by lasts than firsts. We're the last generation to produce and hold on to albums on vinyl, the last generation to read newspapers, the last generation to remember television dials that stopped at thirteen channels, the last generation to express any sort of resistance to corporate servitude, the last generation to produce old-fashioned movie stars (Julia Roberts and Brad Pitt, Will Smith and Angelina Jolie) as opposed to manufactured aristo-cretins and reality-TV clowns, the last generation to care—or so it seems—about the *culture* part of the term *pop culture*.

I think about the way I absorbed media when I was growing up. In the morning I'd get up early for swim practice and my father would be downstairs in the kitchen, imperially bathrobed, with his coffee and his fried eggs and his newspapers. The *Los Angeles Times*, the *Pasadena Star-News*, the *Wall Street Journal*. The sports section, the business section, the arts section, the editorials—shared, jock-eyed over, spread out inkily on the tile counter, goading us into spirited debate and ideological friction even before the sun was up. Tom Brokaw brought us the news on weeknights—Jennings having been deemed "too liberal," and Rather too much of a loon. Sunday evenings ticked along to the godlike clock of *60 Minutes*. If given the opportunity to dine with any celebrity in the world, I suspect my father would have picked Morley Safer.

On weekends even my timid acts of suburban transgression took place within a traditional rubric, a known grid. When it came to all things underground, my Harvard and my Yale was a shack over on Walnut Street—a place called the Poo-Bah Record Shop. Such a home away from home was Poo-Bah's that when you walked up the stoop, under the canopy of trees, and through the front door, you found actual *furniture*. There sat a sofa, rescued from a Salvation Army, its springs creaky and bent. As long as you weren't too germ phobic, you could sit down on the sofa and scan through all the leftist rants in the independent weeklies—Los Angeles used to have a lot of them. You could lean back and gaze up at the vintage album covers that ringed the walls of the store; you could stare at the black-and-white snapshots of somersaulting, stage-diving punks. You could linger for hours, of course, next to the abundant racks of vinyl. *Flip flip flip flip flip*—after you'd done this for a few years, your fingers would develop the same sensory relationship to the skinny ridges of album covers that a Dodger fielder had with his leather glove. You gained a kind of muscle memory.

You watched certain TV programs on certain nights. You listened to the radio. You saw movies in a movie theater. You rented a video at a store. You looked for phone numbers in the phone book, you paid your bills by signing a check, and you consulted a wristwatch for the time of day. To fashion a personal nostalgia out of these habitual memories is perilous, but, looking back now, the environment in which Generation X came of age seems as distant and cornball as the snow-globey images of the nineteenth century that haunted *The Magnificent Ambersons*. Sleigh rides! Trips to the record store! *Oh, the winters were so much colder then! And oh, the music was so much better!* We come from a lost world, it's true, and much of what defines us is our ambivalent stuckness between a hunger for the new and an attachment to the old. Every generation gets a taste of that conflict, of course, but the speed of change these days is forcing Gen X into a state of constant diligence. Fail to upgrade and you start to feel like an isolated Amazonian tribesman.

Flip through some of that old vinyl now and you're likely to find a lot of albums whose very titles seem to embody a spirit of wistful, lethargic, thrift-shoppy disengagement: *Murmur, Daydream Nation, The Chronic, Slanted and Enchanted, Paul's Boutique, Exile in Guyville, Nevermind*. Some of the signpost Gen-X movies of the past fifteen years, both popular and obscure—*Lost in Translation, The*

Cruise, Dazed and Confused, Wedding Crashers, Old School, The 40 Year Old Virgin, Boys Don't Cry, Before Sunrise and *Before Sunset, The Matrix, Swingers, V for Vendetta*—seem to revel in the perversely liberating thrill of being marginalized. Xers shine when expectations are lowered: one of those high-paid boomer career coaches might come to the conclusion that we just, you know, *define success differently.* We expect to be obsolete.

In fact, obsolescence is good business. If you sell cars, selling ten of them to a family over a period of time is much better than selling two. If the car that you sell has a habit of conking out after a few thousand miles, it is not necessarily a disadvantage. A corporation might even plan for it. A corporation might even be inclined to factor such a time line into the engineering. Generation X was programmed for planned obsolescence from the start, but somehow its system has kept on ticking. The X servers are stuffed to the gills, the dial-up connection is too slow, and the operating system feels as quaintly rudimentary as Pong. X should be poisoning a landfill by now. X should be kaput, and it's true that sometimes it feels as though X is chugging along on fumes.

I pick up the *New York Times* and learn that Micawber Books, the old store on Nassau Street in which I used to kill time when I was a student at Princeton, is shutting down. Keep in mind that we're talking about Princeton, New Jersey. *A college town*—maybe the most prototypically Ivy League town in America—and a store that used to stand right across the street from the grand old gates of the college itself. What, do Princeton students no longer like books—or at least the pleasure of a spellbound drift through the shelves? "The driving force of all of this is the acceleration of our culture," Logan Fox, Micawber's owner, muses in the *Times.* "The old days of browsing, the old days of a person coming in for three or four hours on a Saturday and slowly meandering, making a small pile of books, being very selective, coming away with six or seven gems they wanted, are pretty much over." Another day the *Times* has a story about Cody's Books in Berkeley, California. It's closing down, too. "We have a completely different kind of student body than used to go to Berkeley," Marc Weinstein tells the paper. He's the co-owner of Amoeba Music, the Parthenon of American record stores, which sits across Telegraph Avenue from Cody's. Weinstein's own sales have dropped by a third. "What used to be a much more kind of social and politically orientated and active group is now much more business-orientated. There really isn't a passion for art and music the way there used to be."

A few days later I'm standing on Broadway—right on the main artery of the Upper West Side, the storied flank of Manhattan that stretches from Lincoln Center to Columbia University—when I see that Murder Ink and Ivy's Books, the Siamese-twin bookshops that used to specialize in the noir and the twee, are now shuttered behind grates. Murder Ink and Ivy's used to have a mascot, Gus the Dog. A Polaroid of Gus hangs taped to the window—well, the part of the window that you can see under the grate—and a caption on the Polaroid says "1995–2006." The bodega next store has managed to remain open, thanks presumably to the enduring popularity of cigarettes and lottery tickets, and on prominent display in *its* Upper West Side window are belles lettres of a different sort: *Us Weekly* has a cover story on Owen Wilson and Kate Hudson breaking up. *Star* has opted for the purported bifurcation of Justin Timberlake and Cameron Diaz. The cover line for each magazine is the same: IT'S OVER!

No shit it's over. Tower Records on the Sunset Strip? Gone. The headline on the cover of the last issue of the *Los Angeles Alternative*? PRINT IS DEAD. The fabled CBGB? *Hasta luego.* Yes, unbelievable—even CBGB, that grotty Bowery incubator for trillions of Gen-X germs—the club that bred the Ramones, Patti Smith, Talking Heads, and Sonic Youth—*gone.* "It's the cultural rape of New York City that this place is being pushed out," a thirty-six-year-old photographer named John Nikolai told the *New York Times* on the night when CBGB fell victim to the gentrification onslaught. Patti Smith herself called it "a symptom of the empty new prosperity of our city," but the symptoms were by no means confined to Manhattan.

Everywhere you went, the old slacker magnets were shutting down, and the global chain giants were moving in. The situation seemed hopeless, but it wasn't, really, because as Patti pointed out onstage that night, the virus is stubborn. It replicates. It spreads. Bury the infected host body and the bacteriophage will simply leak out into the groundwater. "CBGB is a state of mind," she said. "There's new kids with new ideas all over the world. They'll make their own places—it doesn't matter whether it's here or wherever it is."

X

People like to say that Woodstock changed the world. A few people went back to the garden, poked around in the weeds, and then turned around and drove home to Syosset to practice corporate law. Woodstock didn't change anything other than the composition of some agricultural soil in upstate New York.

The irony is that X *is* changing the world, even though much of the change has occurred in stealth. Xers with a tendency to gaze inward—to fixate on curious microcosms—are bringing about global transformations that are surprisingly outgoing and macro. Google, YouTube, Amazon, Netflix, and Wikipedia have grown fat on a love for free-floating scraps of data. (And *love* is the word for it, considering that flutter of infatuation you feel whenever you type "the Replacements" into YouTube and find yourself watching lost footage of the band tearing through "Bastards of Young" at some pilsner-sticky Hoboken rathskeller.) The dream of Woodstock was to get a lot of people together in a naked group hug, but the X approach "was, and is, a negation of collectivity," as Coupland has written. "Because of this, the moment you use it to describe people in bulk, it fails, and always will." He's right, but technology has given Xers the chance to inhabit "I" and "we" at the same time.

The boomers never came up with anything that approaches the hugeness of Google. John Lennon got bitch-slapped for saying the Beatles were bigger than Jesus, but Google, the brainchild of Gen

Xers Larry Page and Sergey Brin, gives God a run for His money. Google knows everything. How many people live in Bolivia? Ask Google. How far away is Venus? Tell us, O Google. Google sees everything—thanks to the magic of Google Maps, Google can see your own backyard. Google listens to your entreaties; Google is infinite. Google even has a motto that the Supreme Being has got to envy, because it really gets to the point: Don't Be Evil.

Stephen Colbert Saves the World

> There are no exact guidelines. There are probably no guidelines at all. The only thing I can recommend at this stage is a sense of humor, an ability to see things in their ridiculous and absurd dimensions, to laugh at others and at ourselves, a sense of irony regarding everything that calls out for parody in this world.
>
> —*Czech leader Václav Havel, upon receiving the Open Society Prize in 1999 (translated by Paul Wilson)*

> The biggest mistake people make is thinking that Jon and Stephen sit down before every show and say, OK, how are we going to change the world? or any bullshit like that. They both really just want to get a laugh.
>
> —*Ben Karlin, producer of Jon Stewart's* The Daily Show *and Stephen Colbert's* The Colbert Report, *quoted in* Rolling Stone

There's a key scene about two-thirds of the way through *Slacker*. A guy is wearing a sweaty cowboy hat and carrying an armful of books. He wanders—well, everyone in *Slacker* wanders—across the street to a patio. People are milling around on the patio. It's just the kind of prototypical Austin patio, next to the kind of prototypical Austin bungalow, where you'd expect to find off-duty baristi lounging on sun-bleached beach chairs, downing tofu-and-spinach burritos, passing a spliff, talking the Flat Duo Jets and Howard Zinn. The guy in the cowboy hat meets up with the hippie chick in sunglasses. She is riffing about a "total recalibration of my mind." She is holding a deck of cards. She tells the cowboy to pick one. He does, and the first card that he grabs says this: "Withdrawing in disgust is not the same thing as apathy."

Which is such a great line. I know people who haven't seen *Slacker* in years, and they can't really remember any scenes from it, but they can still recite that one line as if it were "Second prize, set of steak knives" or "Show me the money!"

What I didn't know when I first saw *Slacker* in 1992 was that that woman's deck of cards has a pedigree. They aren't just something she hatched on her lunch break down at the anarchist book depot. These Oblique Strategies cards are part of a project created in the mid-seventies by the British painter Peter Schmidt and Brian Eno, the musician and producer behind sonically luxurious signposts like U2's *The Joshua Tree* and Talking Heads' *Remain in Light*. (Which, subsequently, means that they're just what you'd expect the Howard Zinn tofu-and-spinach people to be way into. That's the excellent thing about *Slacker*. The movie's got layers.)

Eno and Schmidt determined that whenever they were working under tremendous pressure, they ran the risk of losing touch with the puckish creative spirit they had when they were slacking. Stress made them rigid and boring. "The Strategies were, then, a way to remind themselves of those habits of thinking—to jog the mind," the writer Gregory Taylor has explained on a site devoted to the method.

Think of Oblique Strategies as sort of a boho Tarot, but instead of picking a card and seeing the future, you see the present. You give your frontal lobes an oil change. Blink, uncoil your brain for a second or two, and all of a sudden the world looks different. Or at least that's the idea. Here are some random atrophy busters in the Eno-Schmidt arsenal:

Discover the recipes you are using and abandon them
Emphasize the flaws
Abandon normal instruments
Turn it upside down

I'm pretty sure that if I were to bring up this Oblique Strategies voo-doo with Jon Stewart and Stephen Colbert, they would smirk me right out of the room. And yet there's no getting around it: when-ever I watch Stewart's and Colbert's *The Daily Show* and *The Colbert Report*, their blasts of political satire on Comedy Central, I feel like I am undergoing a recalibration of my mind. I'm the guy in the cow-boy hat, and I just pulled the card about withdrawing in disgust.

For years now, Stewart and Colbert have been insistent about one thing: They're just comedians. They're not activists. They're not *leaders*. All they want to do is make you laugh, and if millions of people have come to rely on them as a primary source of news, well, *that's insane*, so there's no point in blaming the messenger. "Please don't look to me for information," Colbert once begged a group of smiley and fresh-scrubbed students at Harvard's Kennedy School of Government. "Because sometimes I lie."

Nothing seems to rankle Comedy Central's dyspeptic duo more than when somebody calls them "subversives." You can see why. First of all, it's not so cool to use the word anymore. It's been milked to death. Somewhere on Madison Avenue, right at this mo-ment, there's a fauxhawked and square-toed ad executive cooking up a viral campaign for Starbucks, and he's all torqued up about how "subversive" it is. Second, what real subversive would be enough of a chucklehead to call himself such a thing? Dogma, like Raid, kills the funny on contact. *Yeah, that's right, Colbert and I are secretly using the weapon of humor to undermine repressive social norms and loosen the cor-porate elite's iron grip of power!* Once you've said that, you're fucked.

Besides, the truth is that Stewart and Colbert and their Comedy Central comrades—correspondents Samantha Bee, Larry Wilmore, Rob Corddry, Ed Helms, John Hodgman—don't have much in common with Abbie Hoffman and the hairy gaggle of radical-chic rabble-rousers you associate with the sixties. There's something endearingly and harmlessly square about them. "We are not warriors in anyone's army," Stewart told Maureen Dowd in *Rolling Stone*. "And that is not trying to be self-deprecating. I'm proud of what we do. I really like these two shows. . . . But I understand their place. I don't view us as people who lead social movements." Stephen Colbert is nowhere near as conservative as the clueless and bullying Bill O'Reilly clone he plays on *The Colbert Report*, but neither is he some didgeridoo-droning saboteur. He lives with his wife and kids in the suburbs of New Jersey. He teaches Sunday school at a Catholic church. He's obsessed with *The Lord of the Rings*. He dresses like a pharmaceutical rep from Tallahassee.

And yet, some of the things that Colbert and Stewart say, purely for your amusement, *with absolutely nothing subversive in mind, uh-uh, no way*, well, they're pretty dam subversive. A single offhand gibe of Stewart's can be as pungent and clarifying as turpentine. Add a dab to your nightly television viewing and watch layers of political cant peeling away.

Maybe that's why Colbert's speech at the White House Correspondents' Association dinner on April 29, 2006, outraged and confused so many people. The crowd that night was dense with Beltway wonks and power brokers—the kind of grown-up Tracy Flicks who had their irony glands surgically removed as part of a two-for-one deal back when they got their tonsils out. I'm guessing that a lot of these Georgetown grinds didn't know jack about Stephen Colbert. I suppose they were expecting some Comedy Store quipster cracking wise about airplane food. Instead, this benign, bespectacled, and curiously square minivan dad wanders to the podium from the wilds of basic cable and begins heaping praise on our glorious president. The wonks in the audience—they're not sure why it's funny. They're not even sure what the guy is *doing*. They're used to a different *kind* of party, the kind of party where everybody gets knackered on Stoli and tonics and Karl Rove does the funny fat-white-man-rapping dance and all that ugly friction between the politicians and the press room—between our elected representatives and the well-paid professionals who are supposed to cover them—melts away in a slurry blur of backslapping benevolence. The kind of party where the next day everyone gets to joke about their hangovers.

So, yeah, this must've been confusing. Because the minivan dad's pile of praise—well, it smelled like a compost heap of *mockery*. It was ripe. It was ruthless. Even if you did know Colbert, even if you were up to speed with his TV shtick, well, it was disorienting to realize how *dark* it looked, how *seditious*, with the president of the United States sitting only a few feet away, glowering and pursing his lips. Colbert wore a crisp and traditional tuxedo, and he held the dais for an astonishing twenty-four minutes without being sacked by the Secret Service, but his jag of satire was so precise in its evisceration of the commander in chief that Colbert's accountant was probably readying the paperwork for an IRS audit.

If you watched the footage later, and if you happened to have reached a personal boiling point with all the embarrassments and deceptions and fuckups leaking out of our nation's capital like pus from an infected blister, then it's quite possible that you found Colbert's routine that night to be inspiring, cathartic, *cleansing*. Maybe you hailed Stephen Colbert as a superhero—Irony Man saves the world! Seeing him at that podium was like watching a black-comedy remake of *Mr. Smith Goes to Washington* directed by Alexander Payne, a remake in which Jimmy Stewart's crusading cornball innocent turns into a lobbyist for the League of Gentleman Satirists.

"Guys like us, we're not some brainiacs on the nerd patrol," Colbert told the president. "We're not members of the Factonista. We go straight from the gut—right, sir?" And here Colbert looked, unflinchingly, right into the eyes of the president. "That's where the truth lies. Right down here in the *gut*. Do you know you have more nerve endings in your *gut* than you have in your head? You can look it up. Now I know some of you are going to say, 'I *did* look it up, and that's not true.' That's 'cause you looked it up in a book. Next time look it up in your *gut. I* did. My gut tells me that's how our nervous system works."

He went on: "I believe the government that governs best is the government that governs least, and by these standards we have set up a fabulous government in Iraq."

He went on: "Now I know there are some polls out there saying this man has a 32 percent approval rating. But guys like us, we don't pay attention to the polls. We know that polls are just a collection of statistics that reflect what people are thinking *in reality*, and reality has a well-known liberal bias."

And still he went on: "I stand by this man. I stand by this man because he stands *for* things. Not only *for* things, he stands *on* things. Things like aircraft carriers, and rubble, and recently flooded city squares. And that sends a strong message that no matter what happens to America, she will always rebound with the most powerfully staged photo ops in the world."

Nor would those in the audience be spared.

"Fox News gives you both sides of every story—the president's side and the vice president's side. But the rest of you, what are you *thinking*, reporting on NSA wiretapping or secret prisons in Eastern Europe? Those things are secret for a *very* important reason: they're *superdepressing*. And if that's your goal, well, misery accomplished! Over the last five years, you people were so good! Over tax cuts, WMD intelligence, the effect of global warming, we Americans didn't want to know, and you had the courtesy not to try to find out."

By this point, the laughter in the room had begun to develop a layer of frost. If you watch footage of Colbert's routine, you'll see that he does manage to reveal a slight undercurrent of human affection for the president, even when he's skewering him, but when he gets to the part about the press, he tiptoes right on up to the precipice of fury. "Listen, let's review the rules," Colbert tells them. "Here's how it works. The president makes decisions—he's the Decider. The press secretary announces those decisions, and you people of the press *type* those decisions down. Make, announce, type. Just put 'em through a spell check, and go home. Get to know your family again. Make love to your wife! Write that novel you've got kickin' around in your head. You know, the one about the intrepid Washington reporter with the courage to stand up to the administration! You know, *fiction!*"

X

You know, I learned something today.

—*South Park*

Although Colbert himself would wince at the suggestion, his hilarious act of transgression was a Cooler King moment for the ages, a stroke of Gen-X triumph on a par with the "Smells Like Teen Spirit" video and Quentin Tarantino's Palme d'Or. It played out like an Oblique Strategy on a grand scale: you saw it and—*blam*—you were awakened.

It felt like the first pebble to loosen an avalanche; within days you could pick up the thunder of public opinion as it seemed, finally, to shift en masse. (For years the Republicans had been gearing up for the establishment of a permanent majority in American government, but a few months after the Colbert speech President Bush's party would lose both houses of Congress.) It sent out tremors through the blogosphere for weeks, and it proved, once and for all, that Xers had become much better than the boomers at two things that the bleeding ponytails loved to claim as their own exclusive turf: comedy and protest.

As made clear by Stewart and Colbert and contemporary hit movies like *Wedding Crashers* and *Meet the Parents*, *Old School* and

School of Rock and *Borat: Cultural Learnings of America for Make Benefit Glorious Nation of Kazakhstan*, Gen X rules the comedy world. All that excess irony has come in handy. Maybe our singer-songwriters have become as marginalized as Carthusian monks, but X comedians from the States and England dominate the box office and the tube. Tick off their names—Will Ferrell, Chris Rock, Jack Black, Dave Chappelle, Mike Myers, Steve Carell, Vince Vaughn, Amy Poehler, Maya Rudolph, Margaret Cho, Ben Stiller, Owen Wilson, Molly Shannon, Sarah Silverman, Judd Apatow, George Lopez, Dane Cook, Ze Frank, Conan O'Brien, Tina Fey, Mike Judge, Steve Coogan, Ricky Gervais, Sacha Baron Cohen—and you've got the all-star lampoon-squad equivalent of the Yankees under Casey Stengel.

What's even more striking is that thanks to Xers, we're living through a golden age of political satire. This is a strange and re-markable development. If, as George S. Kaufman famously put it, satire is what closes on Saturday night, then *political* satire is what gets shut down a few minutes after lunch at your desk on Thursday. There persists an assumption that Americans have no stomach for either politics or satire, and yet during the infant years of the twenty-first century the country seemed to clamor for both.

For this we have a boomer to thank. Whether you're a Democrat or a Republican, a Libertarian or a Green, a carnivore or a vegan, or somebody who just can't be bothered, there is one topic about which you can probably agree with your adversaries: George W. Bush. The Bush years have sucked so fantastically, so operatically, and in so many fascinating ways, that people of every political, spiritual, and culinary persuasion have found it hard not to be enraged.

Terrorists attacked New York and Washington, D.C., and London and Madrid. The war in Iraq collapsed into an insoluble catastrophe. Nauseating images of degradation bubbled up from Iraq's Abu Ghraib prison and the Guantánamo Bay naval base. Wounded American soldiers came home to rotten care and bu-reaucratic nightmares. A hurricane savaged a great American city while the White House did nothing. (Well, that's not entirely true. Condoleezza Rice, that avowed shoe nut, dashed into Ferragamo on Fifth Avenue and chuckled herself silly at *Spamalot*.) Day after day brought the erosion of civil liberties, the swelling up of federal deficits, the bursting of a housing bubble, a spinning carousel of scandals and abuses of power.

Plenty of people were quietly seething during the long, gray slog of the Dubya dominion, and they couldn't get much relief by switching on the news—especially when what they found was 24/7 coverage of Britney Spears shaving her head. Protest was futile, or at least that's how it felt. On one hand there was a furious chattering of dissent—blogs! podcasts! viral video!—but on the other hand it was the sterile insect technique all over again: there were so many chattering voices that you couldn't think straight. They cancelled each other out. Aside from ranting and blogging and snarling—well, *what could you do?* Join a march? Carry a picket sign? Oh, for God's sake . . . *chant?*

Fortunately, you could find relief, and recalibration, and *dissent* in some of the most unexpected places. The comedians, it seemed, had a secret plan to keep everybody sane. Lunatic newspaper headlines didn't look the same after you'd spent a few minutes with the *Onion*. A wing-nut Torquemada like Bill O'Reilly turned into a clown as soon as you watched Colbert puncturing all that bilious gasbaggery with his invisible needle. And if you still happened to have any residual reverence for the dismal, drooling celebrity goons of *Us Weekly*, well, *South Park* could cure that in two or three minutes.

The first miracle of *South Park* was that it even existed. The second was that it stayed on the air for more than ten years. (The third was that it spawned an Oscar-nominated movie, 1999's *South Park: Bigger Longer & Uncut*, which featured Saddam Hussein and a talking clitoris. Focus on the Family, the Christian organization, did not hesitate to call it "the vilest film ever.") This was a show—just a nice little Emmy-winning cartoon, available to anyone on normal cable television—whose wholesale slaughter of sacred cows made the climactic scene in *Apocalypse Now* look like a Mennonite square dance. Matt Stone and Trey Parker, the two Xers who'd unleashed the *South Park* pathogen upon the planet in 1997, hailed from Colorado, just like Janice Min and the Columbine killers. From the very start, they seemed to operate on a kitschelimination principle: as soon as that Forrest Gumpy glow began to emanate from anyone in American life, they shot him down.

Parker and Stone began in blasphemy, at the University of Colorado, with a yuletide glue-and-construction-paper short in which the baby Jesus did battle with a demonic Frosty the Snowman. From there they only got sicker; breaking into mainstream television seemed to encourage them to up the ante. They called their pilot episode "Cartman Gets an Anal Probe." Their characters, helium-voiced elementary-school hellions, had a special talent for finding themselves in situations that were guaranteed to offend somebody, anybody, everybody: Catholics and Scientologists, evangelicals and Jews, gays, African Americans, women, animals. Nobody was safe on *South Park*—and that, strangely, gave the show a prophetic kind of moral clarity. If Parker and Stone thought something was bullshit, they said so. They were nobody's ideological lapdogs. They refused to be duped. They acted unreasonably in the name of reason. Yes, *reason*. The scatological vulgarity was smeared so thick on *South Park* that you might've assumed that Stone and Parker had stomped all over their own moral compass a long time ago, but consider this exchange from an interview with Mickey Rapkin in *GQ*:

> **GQ**: You did an episode about Paris Hilton, in which she opens up a retail store called Stupid Spoiled Whore. Why pick on Paris?
>
> **Trey Parker**: Okay, for me, she's a whore. Whatever. She's a dumb, ugly whore. But then I walked into a Guess?

store, and she was all over the place. I'm like, Wait a minute, they're treating her like a glamorous model now? Does anyone notice how dangerous this could be to little girls?

X

"Smells Like Teen Spirit" didn't happen overnight. It represented the culmination of hundreds of underground bands inching closer and closer to a mainstream breakthrough. In the same way, Stephen Colbert's spectacular moral triumph at the White House Correspondents' Association dinner had a history. Everybody referred to Jon Stewart as "the most trusted name in fake news," but he was by no means the first. Fake news had ruled as the primary mode of Gen-X comedy for a couple of decades or so. In the late eighties students at the University of Wisconsin–Madison created the *Onion*, a newspaper that ingeniously parodied the idiocy of American news gathering, and, by the middle of the nineties, when the *Onion* launched a Web site and went fully national, sharing absurd headlines from the *Onion* was a dependable way to fritter away a day at the office. Among the standouts:

COLUMBINE JOCKS SAFELY RESUME BULLYING

U.S. POPULACE LURCHES METHODICALLY THROUGH THE
MOTIONS FOR YET ANOTHER DAY

TRANSGENDERED SEA ANEMONE DENOUNCED AS
"ABOMINATION" BY CLERGY

CHRIST CONVERTS TO ISLAM

MARILYN MANSON NOW GOING DOOR-TO-DOOR TRYING
TO SHOCK PEOPLE

Maybe the most telling of the *Onion*'s forays into social commentary was this one, headlined CONGRESS PASSES FREEDOM FROM INFORMATION ACT:

> WASHINGTON, DC—Calling the unregulated flow of information "the single greatest threat to the emotional comfort and well-being of the American people," Congress passed the Freedom From Information Act Monday. The legislation—a response to widespread public demand to know less about the realities of the world—guarantees citizens protection from unpleasant information and imposes tough new restrictions on facts that federal authorities deem potentially damaging to the public's peace of mind.

"Irony" is usually the first word that people blurt out when anyone mentions Generation X. There's a fair amount of guilt attached to this. The Xer is aware that he or she is skilled at making fun of everything and is simultaneously concerned that this skill contributes zilch when it comes to changing or improving the things that he or she is making fun of. But ask yourself: What's more effective, a picket sign or an expertly calibrated joke?

If there's one piece of history that boomers love to shove in our faces as evidence that they haven't left the world in tatters, it's their expertise at organized protest. *We took to the streets, maaaan! We brought the gears of power to a standstill! We ended a freakin' war!* The problem is, the boomers refused to march unless they could do so while banging on bongo drums and wearing sandals, which guaranteed that for decades a perfectly sensible portion of the Bill of Rights—the right to peaceful assembly—would be inextricably associated with unpleasant aromas. Yeah, maybe all those hippies stopped the Vietnam War. Or maybe they helped *extend* the war for as long as was militarily endurable because nobody in the government wanted to capitulate to an army of Haight-Ashbury Hacky

Sackers. "You go to some anti-war march, there's always some white college kid with blue dreadlocks and a bone through his nose, and of course he's going to be the public face of the protest, so the next day that's going to be the color photo on the top of the *New York Times*," says political cartoonist David Rees. "And some guy in Iowa sees that image and says, 'Well, you know, I don't know how I feel about the war, but I know I can't agree with whatever this freak is marching for.' Everybody should dress up in Brooks Brothers and J. Crew when they go to a march."

If the hippies stigmatized the practice of standing up to The Man, the Brooks Brothers satirists have stepped in to make it effective again. Irony has given Xers crafty new styles of protest that also happen to be highly entertaining. Consider the Yes Men, a team of hide-in-plain-sight hoaxers who dress up like corporate drones and infiltrate prestigious seminars around the world. What's amazing about the Yes Men is that they can step up to a podium, or in front of a cable-news camera, and promulgate some of the most ludicrously Swiftian programs and positions you've ever heard in your life—that slavery is a supertool for growth, that national parks should be opened up to rampant tract-home development, that CEOs should be encased in inflatable SurvivaBalls to protect them from natural disasters brought on by global warming, that people in Third World countries could overcome starvation by eating burgers made out of recycled human shit—and *people will take them totally seriously*. Which, of course, proves their point.

Or take the Billionaires for Bush, the prank artists who chip away at the philosophy of social Darwinism not by chanting and marching against it but by *supporting* it. Dandified in tuxedos and ball gowns, cruising around in stretch limos, brandishing croquet mallets and champagne flutes, equipped with pseudonyms like Phil T. Rich and Dee Forestation, the Billionaires manage to erode the right wing by slapping mock versions of its most cherished maxims across picket signs: "Widen the Income Gap." "Blood for Oil." "Re-Elect Rove." "Billionaires for Bush is a grassroots network of corporate lobbyists, decadent heiresses, Halliburton CEOs, and other winners under George W. Bush's economic policies," the organization crows on its Web site. "Headquartered in Wall Street and with over 60 chapters nationwide, we'll give whatever it takes to ensure four more years of putting profit over people. After all, we know a good president when we buy one." Maybe it's uncool to use a word like *subversive* these days, but in a photo gallery on the site, members of Billionaires for Bush can be seen schmoozing with Donald Rumsfeld and Newt Gingrich, who seem to have absolutely no clue what's going on. Which, again, proves their point.

X

Not long ago David Rees wrote that "my career as a political cartoonist literally began the night I asked myself, 'What would D. Boon do?' before clumsily trying to make the comic-strip equivalent of a Minutemen song." D. Boon was the firebrand at the mike in the Minutemen, the influential agit-punk trio from Los Angeles. He died in 1985 when his van crashed in Arizona, but Rees had D. Boon's ferocity in mind as he tried to come up with a way to react to the aftermath of the 9/11 attacks.

His first response, of course, was to shop. "We all just went to the mall. I did," Rees says. "My wife and I went to the mall and I bought sweatpants and went to Foot Locker to help fight the war on terrorism. Now looking back, it's like, What the fuck was I thinking?" Eventually, Rees found himself feeling so helpless and frustrated that he started to crank out *Get Your War On,* a bitterly hilarious comic strip in which office drones engage in sarcastic-absurdist chitchat. (Sample line: "Oh my God, this War on Terrorism is gonna *rule*! I can't wait until the war is over and there's no more terrorism!") Rees patched together the strips in private, with snippets of clip art. But pretty soon his friends had e-mailed them all over the place, and *Get Your War On* had attracted enough of a cult following that editors began to publish the strips regularly in *Rolling Stone*. "The comic was just one part of this big pop culture that over the years has kind of turned against the Bush doctrine," Rees says. "It's like a really small ripple in that big pond."

Even though *Get Your War On* has been a useful angst catalyst for its fans, Rees himself has been nagged by the thought that giving people a funny way to vent their frustration in a time of emerging global cataclysm isn't, um, *enough*. "Sometimes I think, *Oh my God, this really is the major struggle of my generation. I need to do something, either to help out—or to put an end to it if it is a bunch of BS*. That usually involves spending three hours reading talkingpointsmemo.com," he says. "If this truly is a battle of good versus evil that could last forever, maybe we should do something other than just hitting refresh on our favorite weblogs."

He goes on, "I try to tell myself, 'Well, Dave, you're doing your part, you're making this comic, you're speaking truth to power,' but really, that's a bunch of bullshit. It's not like wearing fifty pounds of body armor in 120-degree heat." Which is why, when the outbursts were collected in a couple of *Get Your War On* books, Rees decided to contribute the profits to a charity that clears land mines in Afghanistan. "That was a way for me to compensate for the helplessness I felt," he says. "I thought, *The comic isn't enough*."

The Sundown Schoolhouse Saves the World

Inhale lift your right leg off the mat exhale bring your right leg up and under to your chest inhale swing your leg back exhale stretch your toes outward while spinning your skull around 360 degrees and wrapping your pancreas into a bow with your spleen . . .

My arms quiver. My ankles wobble. Threads of sweat dribble down my cheeks. Every cell in my body is shot through with agony and confusion, and I collapse into a jellied heap at the very moment when I hear Carol, our yoga instructor, ask the group, "How many of you have experience with headstands?"

Since I keep wondering what happened to a generation of alternative thinkers, I figure it makes sense to find some. Which is how I end up in Los Angeles one October morning, propped up on all fours under a geodesic dome, trying to bend my leg back around like the tail of a scorpion. I've come to the Sundown Schoolhouse, a sort of fringe-power immersion course for adults, and our day has begun with yoga. I've never done yoga. Thanks to the demands of work and parenting, I have no time for any exercise whatsoever, which means that my muscles have all the bendy puissance of overcooked linguini.

Our master of ceremonies, and the guy who owns the geodesic dome, is Fritz Haeg. At thirty-seven, Fritz is something of a freethinking guru about town—architect, teacher, *saloniste*, instigator, activist, bountifully charming party host, promoter of original modes of building and gardening—and the Sundown Schoolhouse represents the essence of his approach to the world. "It is founded on the premise that as artists, designers, performers and writers, we should be powerful and active agents in society," he explains on his site. "We want to look head-on as our natural and urban environments gradually deteriorate around us. We want to invert the power structure as design and the arts are co-opted as tools for marketing. . . . We want to reclaim the promise of art as the ultimate form of human freedom and expression in a society where it has become either trivialized as entertainment, hijacked as pure commodity, under-valued or even feared."

Nine students come to Fritz's house every Tuesday, from 8:00 a.m. to 8:00 p.m., for twelve Tuesdays in a row. They climb the spiral staircase to the dome, where they engage from dawn to dusk in a free-ranging conversation about the state of the world. Most of the students are in their late twenties, at the tail end of the X demo, and it's a diverse group: Alia, Pablo, Qusai, Sarah, Katie, Devin, Mark, Michael, and Tracy.

From the outside, the Sundown Schoolhouse looks like a lost episode of *The Real World* cooked up by Noam Chomsky and

Federico Fellini. But the Schoolhouse is by no means Haeg's only project. He's also the force behind Edible Estates, an initiative that's teaching home owners how to replace their 40 million acres of front lawns with thriving, blooming gardens. Haeg calls it "an attack on the American front lawn and everything it has come to represent," and he fired his first shot across the bow on the Fourth of July 2005, when he and a home-owning couple named Stan and Priti Cox dug up the Cox's suburban lawn in Salina, Kansas, and converted it into a dense botanical oasis. Haeg never sent out a press release about the project, but word of mouth spread, especially through the Web, and by now he's overseeing the planting of Edible Estates gardens from New Jersey to Austin to the Tate Modern in London.

Haeg has been teaching college classes in architecture, art, and design for over a decade—at the Parsons School of Design in New York, the Art Center College of Design in Pasadena, the California Institute of Arts in Valencia, and the University of Southern California—but art and education seem to take up every minute of his private time, too. The bottom half of his house is laid out like a vast medieval wine cave, and he uses the space as a magnet for "events, happenings, gatherings, meetings, pageantry, performances, shows, stunts & spectacles." Attend one of his Sundown Salons and you might stumble into a dance recital, a poetry reading, a lesson in "pastry sculpting," or a performance by a squadron of gay acrobats.

I first meet up with Haeg at a café in Echo Park. He's tall and lean, with a shaved head, an aquiline nose, and a straight-backed, gangly gait that calls to mind a scarecrow at a Buddhist monastery. "American society today is a total mess," he says. "I'm so profoundly disturbed by it on so many levels. What bothers me is people silently and without question accepting the most insane aspects of our culture." What's quintessentially X about Haeg is the way he's chosen to attack the mess. The mere idea of a "movement" makes him cringe. Terms like *rebel* and *counterculture* and *environmentalist* have become old and hollow and useless, he says, and he has little interest in coining new terms to categorize what he's doing. "If there's anything we're fighting against in this culture," he says, "it's the idea that there's only one way, one path."

On the afternoon we meet at the café, Haeg is hosting an Edible Estates lecture next door at the Machine Project. The lecture draws a crowd that spills out onto Alvarado Street, and the message is pretty simple: instead of wasting time and money fussing over a glistening suburban lawn, which does nothing but guzzle down gallons of water and chemicals, home owners should use their land to grow things they can eat. Fritz introduces a guy who's done just that—a computer programmer in his mid-thirties named Michael Foti. If you're walking past the plot in front of Foti's house in Lakewood, you'll find a suburban microjungle bursting with squash, peppers, kumquats, purple sage, Brandywine tomatoes, and white beauty eggplants. Foti and his wife, Jennifer, have grown more food than they can handle—enough to supply the whole neighborhood. They're teaching themselves and their two daughters about canning and pickling—"things," Michael says, "that our grandmothers knew how to do."

This is a prime example of the Fritz Haeg mission. It's also a fitting illustration of the way Xers are quietly, modestly, locally saving the world. "I'm not interested in big monuments," Haeg has said. "I'm interested in singular gestures that become models—small gestures in response to common issues that can be instituted by anyone." Which means you're not going to find him teaming up with Bob Geldof, Celine Dion, and Dr. Phil to host a Get Back to the Garden rock festival. He prefers to keep things small. Besides, "get back to the garden" is a typical boomerish sentiment—sweeping, grandiose, totally impossible. Fritz Haeg just wants you to plant one.

This, too, is what Haeg hopes to accomplish with the Sundown Schoolhouse: not to inflict a prechewed agenda on each of his captive pupils, but simply to encourage them to tear up that bland expanse of green headspace and plant some seeds. Teachers drop by during the course of the day—artist Emily Roysdon, community activist Marc Herbst—but the real lessons come from the way the students interact. They teach each other. Sometimes Qusai Kathawala, a design student originally from India, leads the yoga lessons, and Michael Parker, the group's speed-talking organic food zealot, has a habit of commandeering the meals. Today, we're nibbling on crackers made out of flax, sunflower, and sesame seeds. Parker made the crackers at home, and he went out early this morning to scour the Los Angeles farmers' markets for fresh figs, pears, watermelons, French plums, and obscure varieties of fruit—pineapple guavas and jujubes, for instance. When lunch rolls around, we amble outside to a picnic table, where Michael instructs everyone to stuff lettuce leaves with raw vegetables, squeeze in a few chunks of avocado, and smear the whole loamy envelope with a pungent paste of French sea salt, olive oil, and raw minced garlic. "We eat insanely healthy here," Haeg says. *Insane* is an apt word for it. The next day my digestive system will find itself in the throes of a violent revolution.

But the main thing that strikes me about the Sundown Schoolhouse is simply that Fritz Haeg is doing it in the first place: here he is inviting nine people over to his own house once a week, for twelve hours at a stretch, so that they can sit around introducing each other to new ways of thinking. This, in and of itself, seems like a radical use of his time. When lunch is over, he tells his students that he wants them each to write down a personal manifesto and read it out loud. Look around Los Angeles, he says, and you'll see decisions. Traffic, smog, sprawl—the city feels the way it does because once upon a time, certain people established goals and set out to achieve them. "We're living in the middle of what people decided," Haeg says. These days, the real masters of the art of the manifesto come from the business world. Corporations adore mission statements. Senior staffers at a Fortune 500 company will spend hours in committee, ruthlessly boiling down the syntax of a mission statement until it turns into a roux of pure revenue-generating focus. But whenever the bohemians try to do it, they have a habit of fogging up the windows with gassy jargon—*community, empowerment, otherness, opening up a dialogue*—all that sensitive, posturing stuff that used to get you laid in college.

If the young congregants of the Schoolhouse want things to be different, Haeg says, they need to be clear about what they want. They need to come right out and say it. He brings up the titanically influential architect Le Corbusier, whose *Towards a New Architecture* blasted open a new space for modernism in 1923.

"He had a manifesto?" asks Qusai.

"Oh God, yeah!" says Haeg, leaning back against the wall of the geodesic dome. "He was hard-core. You read it and you imagine him screaming with his fist in the air."

Don't Be Evil

You see, dear reader, so much of what's doled out as punk merely amounts to saying I suck, you suck, the world sucks, and who gives a damn—which is, er, ah, somehow *insufficient*.

—*Lester Bangs*

As the corporate ogre expands its creeping influence on the minds of industrialized youth, the time has come for the International Rockers of the World to convene in celebration of our grand independence.

—*From a poster for the 1991 International Pop Underground Convention in Olympia, Washington*

One day late in August 2005, Cameron Sinclair gazed across a beach in Pottuvil, Sri Lanka. With him was a man named Ashan. Ashan had lost seventeen members of his family in the tsunami that had ravaged villages around the Indian Ocean a few months earlier, and Sinclair was talking with Ashan about ways to rebuild homes on the Arugam Bay. "We were sitting on the beach together," Sinclair says, "which in Sri Lanka is a very eerie feeling, because you've got water coming at you."

Things were about to get eerier. During a pause in the conversation, Sinclair checked his Trēo. At that moment, on a demolished beach thousands of miles away from the Big Easy, he realized that an entirely different shore was about to be clobbered: Hurricane Katrina was bearing down on Louisiana and Mississippi. "We saw the data," he says. "We saw it coming. We said, 'Okay, this is a big one.' " Back in the States his wife, Kate Stohr, caught a flight to the Gulf Coast. And there on the sand in Sri Lanka, Cameron Sinclair tried to keep up with the hundreds of e-mails that were pouring in to his handheld: *How can we get involved?* they asked. *What can we do? I need help.*

The miraculous thing was, Sinclair *could* help—even from a place as remote as Pottuvil. Merely by pecking away at his Trēo, he could raise money, rally architects who might be able to design new houses for decimated neighborhoods, mobilize community leaders. Simply by posting a plea for money on a site like World Changing or BoingBoing, he could ignite a chain reaction, watching his words leapfrog virally from blog to blog—a save-the-world relay in real time. "That's the speed and power of the Internet," he says. "We didn't do any advertising. No celebrities. We raised ten thousand dollars in twenty-three hours. And within three months we'd raised half a million dollars."

Sinclair and Stohr are the founders of an organization called Architecture for Humanity. Where there is extreme poverty or war, or where a natural disaster has struck, Architecture for Humanity steps in to see that uprooted and impoverished people have a place to live. A decent place—maybe even a beautiful place. The way Stohr and Sinclair envision it, moldy FEMA trailers, flimsy toolsheds, reconstituted slums—the "heckuva job Brownie" approach to a catastrophe—will not do. Architecture for Humanity brings something quintessentially X to the mission of helping people: an emphasis on aesthetics. They're do-gooders with good taste. "When you build ugly housing, it depreciates in value at such a rapid rate that there's a loss in it," Sinclair tells me one morning over a bowl of oatmeal and bananas. "This is something I learned from India: When you build something that is beautiful, the community maintains it. People will have pride in where they're living. If you give someone crap, they're going to treat it like crap."

The organization has helped build a medical training center in Tanzania, a sports facility for kids in South Africa, temporary shelters for the survivors of Hurricane Emily on the island of Grenada and for survivors of the 2005 earthquake in Kashmir, and new homes for families in Biloxi, Mississippi, whose houses were gutted by Katrina. These are not prefab tissue-paper huts. They're sturdy, even visually beguiling structures, and they've been dreamed up by professional architects who've often spent weeks lending an ear to the locals to see what kind of design would make the most sense. Stohr and Sinclair subscribe to the idea of "urban acupuncture": pierce a place with one small, dramatic pinpoint improvement, they say, and it engenders a ripple effect.

Sinclair's no stranger to ripple effects. The morning I meet him, the guy has no luggage. Delta Air Lines lost all his bags during his trip from San Francisco to Minneapolis to New York. Within hours he'll be on a flight to Amsterdam. From there, he'll fly to Cape Town, South Africa. From there, he'll catch a smaller plane to Durban. And from there, he'll drive four hours up to the Mozambique border to visit a dirt-poor area where Architecture for Humanity is building an HIV/AIDS clinic. He is about to make this journey without a Dopp kit or a change of clothes, but he doesn't seem the least bit distressed. Ruddy and blond, with a faint trace of his ancestral Scots accent, at thirty-three Sinclair comes off like a modern incarnation of one of the jolly Highland warriors from *Braveheart*. "My nickname, which is now my job title, is Eternal Optimist," he tells me. "You know, you spend a week living on the foundations of somebody's house in Sri Lanka, and they're dealing with digging out their family members, and you're dealing with, like, 'Did I bring my charger for my phone?' It's a little bit of a reality check."

Of course, he doesn't really *need* luggage. He can, with a little acrobatic thumb work on his Trēo, set things in motion that will improve the lives of thousands. This turns out to be a trademark of the new noblesse oblige. While the aging boomer Aquarians tend to get mired in nostalgia for the bongo drums of the past—they can't seem to switch off that flower power newsreel—pioneers like Sinclair are changing the approach altogether. That phrase "urban acupuncture"—well, it's a handy metaphor for the whole Gen-X approach to problem solving: fix things in the microcosm and let your idea radiate outward. Aim high but start small. "The problem with the boomer generation," Sinclair says, "is they really believed in utopia. And utopia is dead."

"Utopia is dead." It's a strange sentiment to hear from a do-gooder, and yet it makes bracing, refreshing sense. "Most people of my generation understand crisis, right?" Sinclair goes on. "So when Al Gore comes out with *An Inconvenient Truth*, most of us, we're like, 'Yeah, tell us something we don't know.' We were *born with this*. We were born with AIDS. We were born with climate issues. We understand crisis. So we're pissed off, and we understand that utopia doesn't work."

Sinclair doesn't believe in perfecting the world. He doesn't expect to march, fists clenched and chin upraised, at the forefront of some grand global movement that will, in one fell swoop, eliminate poverty and liberate the masses. He believes in the small-batch microbrew approach to doing good—*urban acupuncture*—and he believes, also, in what he's fond of calling "the YouTube mentality." The way he sees it, people now have a distribution system for their wild-hair ideas—a plugged-in, decentralized, democratic, interconnected, YouTubing grid that allows anybody's small-batch solution to whip around the globe in ten seconds. In the end, Sinclair says, "what you need is not one solution, but *a hundred million solutions*."

Sinclair has made something of a sport out of questioning the establishment. When he was a high school kid in the English town of Bath, he dug up a newspaper clip listing the ten worst buildings in the city. For centuries Bath had prided itself on being a jewel of the Georgian style, but architects who subscribed to the new brutalist movement in the sixties had arguably ruined the place. Sinclair was determined to smoke out these deluded Howard Roarks of the Cotswolds. "I said, 'I'm going to track down the architects who designed these buildings and ask them why they did this to the city,'" Sinclair says. "Imagine some sixteen-year-old punk coming around to your office going, 'Dude, you destroyed our city and everyone hates you. Why did you do this?'" A few years later, when Sinclair put together a postgraduate thesis devoted to creating shelters for the homeless people of New York, an advisor told him that the topic was "really depressing."

He bought a one-way ticket to New York. He socked away cash while working as an architect in Manhattan, and in 1999 he and Stohr launched Architecture for Humanity. They worked at night, on weekends; eventually Sinclair quit his job. They lived in a 300-square-foot studio, and that doubled as an office: in the daylight hours they crammed five people into it. The building's super jerry-rigged Internet access for them. "It was crazy," Sinclair says. "It was great." Pretty soon, they published a book called *Design Like You Give a Damn*, and Sinclair was taking home honors like the TED Prize and the Lewis Mumford Award for Peace. Eventually, the couple moved west—to Sausalito, California—and watched their small-batch humanitarian project mushroom into an international phenomenon.

In spite of that, Sinclair so far hasn't displayed any signs of Hands Across America megalomania. He and Stohr employ only four people in Architecture for Humanity's office in Sausalito, but they have thousands of architects and designers around the world lined up to volunteer their time. Sinclair Xishly refuses to see himself as the top dog in some hierarchy. His dream is to "open source" the whole freaking thing—just give it away. If you want to start an

Architecture for Humanity chapter in Topeka, his instructions are: *go right ahead, download all the mission statements and blueprints you want.* You don't need his permission. "Just start a chapter," he says. "Go drinking and come up with an idea and do it. I gave away the keys to the castle." He doesn't see Architecture for Humanity as a rigid institution. He sees it as a virus. "If we give these things away, they spread like wildfire," he says. "The ideas get replicated."

Not long ago Sinclair launched something called the Open Architecture Network so that nonprofit groups with the same goals in mind—*build better stuff for people in need*—could find each other online and swap contacts and blueprints. Just as Jon Stewart and Stephen Colbert's barrage of smart bombs on Comedy Central has done more to reveal the buffoonery of the White House and Capitol Hill than a thousand of the boomers' *panna cotta* peace-train sing-alongs, this network of designers and activists, Sinclair says, has the potential to dwarf the relief efforts of the United Nations. "UN-Habitat came out with this big, bold statement: 'We're going to improve the living standards of 100 million people by 2020,'" he says. "I came out with a statement saying, 'I'm going to improve the living standards of 5 *billion* people.'"

X

In January 1984, Apple created a wave of buzz for its new Macintosh computer by airing a commercial during the Super Bowl. By now it's revered as one of the most influential spots in the history of advertising. In the ad, which was directed by *Blade Runner*'s Ridley Scott, thousands of dutiful and brain-numbed proles marched into an auditorium to listen to a lecture. "Today, we celebrate the first glorious anniversary of the Information Purification Directives," their fearless leader droned on, haranguing them from a giant screen. "We have created, for the first time in all history, a garden of pure ideology. Where each worker may bloom secure from the pests of contradictory and confusing truths." As the lecture went on, a sporty blond woman—because of those orange shorts of hers, I've always imagined her moonlighting as a waitress at Hooters—bolted rebelliously into the auditorium and hurled a sledgehammer at the screen.

Twenty-three years later, in the spring of 2007, U.S. senator and presidential candidate Barack Obama basked in an efflorescence of buzz thanks to a viral Web commercial that came right out and copied Apple's sixty-second opus. The Obama ad, which racked up millions of hits on YouTube, looked exactly the same as the Orwellian Apple one, except that the voice and face of the fearless leader belonged to Hillary Clinton. Obama's camp didn't commission the spot—officially, they had nothing to do with it—but they had to be grateful. The ad expressed something that no American politician could say out loud: after fifteen years of Bubba and Dubya, boomer politics was in danger of crossing the line into kitsch.

When Obama talks about finally moving on from "the psychodrama of the baby boom generation—a tale rooted in old grudges and revenge plots hatched on a handful of college campuses long ago," it's an open invitation to the next wave. Obama was born in August 1961, just days after Richard Linklater and a few months before Douglas Coupland. Scan his first book, *Dreams from My Father*, and you'll see that Obama's way of thinking developed amid the backwash of skepticism that followed the grand march of the sixties and seventies. He's allergic to anything that smacks of movementism. When he writes about his days at Occidental College in California at the start of the eighties, he does so with the cool, Couplandesque eye of a skilled social anthropologist. "To avoid being mistaken for a sellout, I chose my friends carefully," Obama says in the book. "The more politically active black students. The foreign students. The Chicanos. The Marxist professors and structural feminists and punk-rock performance poets. We smoked cigarettes and wore leather jackets. At night, in the dorms, we discussed neocolonialism, Franz Fanon, Eurocentrism, and patriarchy. When we ground out our cigarettes in the hallway carpet or set our stereos so loud that the walls began to shake, we were resisting bourgeois society's stifling constraints. We weren't indifferent or careless or insecure. We were alienated."

In one of the most fascinating parts of *Dreams from My Father*—and one of the most honest passages you'll ever see in a book written by a politician—Obama talks about addressing a crowd at a college rally against South African apartheid. Up at the podium he delivers something that's part sermon and part skit: he's staged it so that when he's one minute into the speech, a couple of white students will accost him and usher him away from the microphone—this to make a point about the squelching of free speech in South Africa. Obama speaks well, powerfully, and so do some friends who follow him at the mike, but then he steps back and finds himself annoyed by the narcissistic pageantry of the scene. "I should have been proud of the two of them; they were eloquent, you could tell the crowd was moved," he writes,

> but I wasn't really listening anymore. I was on the outside again, watching, judging, skeptical. Through my eyes, we suddenly appeared like the sleek and well-fed amateurs we were, with our black chiffon armbands and hand-painted signs and earnest young faces. The Frisbee players had returned to their game. When the trustees began to arrive for their meeting, a few of them paused behind the glass walls of the administration building to watch us, and I noticed the old white men chuckling to themselves, one old geezer even waving in our direction. The whole thing was a farce, I thought to myself—the rally, the banners, everything. A pleasant afternoon diversion, a school play without the parents. And me and my one-minute oration—the biggest farce of all.

It's hard to imagine that kind of self-doubt coming from the Clintons, who seem to have mythologized every "Chelsea

Morning" moment in their lives. Actually, it's hard to imagine *any* major boomer politician from the left having the guts to come out and admit that one of the antiwar be-ins of the sixties was little more than an exercise in ego-tripping. Doubt of this sort seems not to have paralyzed Barack Obama. He's running for president. Whether or not he wins, maybe his brand of pragmatic optimism— postideological, steeped in history, skilled at the art of bullshit detection—represents an example of how the X perspective can flourish on the national stage.

By 2007 Obama was probably the most prominent Xer who'd found a way to reconcile his ironic wariness with an impulse to save the world, but he was by no means the only one. Consider Cory Booker, the young mayor who was trying to summon up a renaissance amid the weed-patch battlefields of Newark, New Jersey. Consider Majora Carter, who grew up playing in the burned-out tenements of the South Bronx and moved back, after earning degrees from Wesleyan College and New York University, to "green the ghetto." Sustainable South Bronx, the organization that she founded in 2001, lobbies aggressively and craftily for the creation of riverside parks, greenways, and blooming floral roofs in a neighborhood of New York that tends to get the shaft when it comes to anything involving "quality of life." "We're the poorest congressional district in the whole country, and I'm really getting tired of that designation," Carter says. "It's been that way for twenty years. Early on, I don't think people knew what to do with someone like me, because in my neighborhood there were no trees to hug." Carter's work landed her a MacArthur Foundation "genius" fellowship in 2005, and if you speak with her for even just a few minutes you'll notice that she does not shrink from the notion of saving the world. "I absolutely say that, and I don't mean it in any ironic sense," Carter tells me. "This is a very deliberate thing that I do. It has to be audacious, and it has to be kind of big, because otherwise nobody will take it seriously. I am idealistic enough to really believe that through the fruits of my labor, people's lives *are* going to be changed. I'm not doing this just because I think green is pretty."

On the surface, yeah, I suppose a proposition like "X saves the world" is preposterous. I like it *because* it's preposterous. I think it makes a bizarre kind of sense—only a small and quiet and marginalized demographic has the will to preserve things that are small and quiet and marginalized in the world. The boomers and the millennials have always been much bigger and louder population clumps. Both swell past the 70 million mark, whereas Generation X is usually pegged at around 46 million. By numbers alone we're probably condemned to nicheville. The question is whether *nicheville* might just be another word for—as Cameron Sinclair puts it— "a hundred million solutions."

Nicheville itself can be a solution in a monocultural world. Right now, in the same way that Fritz Haeg is launching an assault on the "toxic uniformity" of suburban lawns, hundreds of riot grrrls–turned–mommy bloggers and Stitch 'n Bitch knitters are doing their damnedest to blast the Stepford-style drudgery out of domesticity. Consider Isa Chandra Moskowitz, the host of a vegan cooking show called *The Post Punk Kitchen*. "Punk taught me to question everything," she tells the *New York Times*. "Of course, in my case that means questioning how to make a Hostess cupcake without eggs, butter, or cream." Take Leah Kramer, who left steady work in computer programming in 2003 and embarked on Craftster.org, a DIY site devoted to people who have a campy Martha-Stewart-with-a-mohawk obsession with sewing, knitting, making art out of discarded soda cans, and dyeing Easter eggs with, say, the Black Flag logo. (The site's slogan: "No tea cozies without irony.") By 2007 it had almost 100,000 members.

X

"We have a small restaurant on Rivington Street, and we have a small drinks company, and, let's face it, we're small people," says

Moby. Moby doesn't say that in a song but (in conjunction with his business partner, Kelly Tisdale) on the back label of a bottle of his vanilla berry hibiscus tea. That's what Moby did after his album *Play* became the soundtrack for every Gen-X cocktail party in America—he went and launched Teany, a line of healthy herbal teas. You can see where things lead from here. You imagine Moby taking the proceeds from Teany, going back to school for a degree in the healing arts, and opening up a cozy spa and bed-and-breakfast on the outskirts of Santa Fe.

MobySpa will offer everything—aromatherapy, seaweed wraps, tai chi—and will cater to all those rich, frazzled millennials who need an escape from their busy lives. One day, decades from now, Paris Hilton will show up at MobySpa, unannounced, cradling a lemur and wearing a pink T-shirt that says "I'm a fucking survivor!" Moby, dressed in a saffron robe, will slowly walk the polished stones of the MobySpa labyrinth to greet her. He will look exactly the same as he does now. Healthy living! Peace in marginalization! Paris will look like Marianne Faithfull—haggard, narcoleptic, smeared—and yet somehow smooth and shiny, too, thanks to $20 million worth of nanobiotic cosmetic treatments. Still, she'll be . . . tired. Spent. Confused. Moby will detect this. Moby will bring her a nice, calming cup of chamomile pomegranate tea, and Paris will sit under the sun and survey the modest, piñon-dotted grounds. "Oh my God, it's so peaceful here," she'll say. "Oh my God, I'm sure you never miss those terrible New York parties."

I suppose it's easy to imagine Generation X slipping into a sort of sleepy-backwater oblivion. It'll probably take an avian flu outbreak to make the boomers give up the limelight. During the summer of 2006 *Fortune* published a story titled "Have You Outgrown Your Job?" The writer, Anne Fisher, interviewed a variety of Gen Xers in corporate jobs who kept slamming up against the "gray ceiling." These thirtysomething bankers and account managers had decent, well-paying jobs, but there was one glitch: immobility. The Xers couldn't move up. The ladder was gridlocked. The toniest executive-washroom slots belonged to boomers, and those boomers (*your generation is not headed for bingo night!*) had no intention of budging. *Ever.* Retire? Shit, these intransigent ponytails would have to be wheeled out in tie-dyed coffins. "Fifteen-hour days have become the norm. Untethering oneself from one's BlackBerry is, in many fields, considered high treason. And weekends? Those are for catching up on e-mail, right? All this might not be so terrible if that big promotion—the one that catapults an up-and-comer out of middle-management hell and into the senior ranks—were around the corner. But increasingly, younger workers are finding that no matter how many hours they put in or how much their bosses rave about their work, they're just plain stuck. An entire generation is bumping against something no amount of youthful vigor can match," Fisher wrote. "Generation X, it would seem, is in danger of turning into the Prince Charles of the American workforce: perpetual heirs apparent awaiting the keys to the kingdom."

That may be true in the principalities of Khaki and Bluetooth, but plenty of Xers continue to plant their flags in rogue colonies of their own—*on* their own. Dave Eggers, the editor of McSweeney's and the author of *A Heartbreaking Work of Staggering Genius*, has hatched his own method of urban acupuncture. After all his success selling books and editing magazines, Eggers opened up 826 Valencia in San Francisco's Mission district. At first glance it appeared to be (*ha*) a pirate supply store—an ironic emporium for eye patches, spyglasses, Jolly Roger flags, and swashbuckling accoutrements of that ilk—but in fact 826 Valencia turns out to be a nonprofit writing center where local kids can find tutors and attend free workshops. The 826 franchise has wound up spreading to Los Angeles, Seattle, Chicago, Brooklyn, Ann Arbor, and Boston.

Consider Tim Westergren, whose Music Genome Project uses an algorithm to chip away at the *High School Musical* monoculture of the masses. Westergren has figured out how to break a piece of music down to snippets of elemental code, like strands of DNA.

Visit Pandora, the Internet radio service he's built up out of these sonic-genetic patterns, and you'll feel like you're sliding your fingers into a huge musical hive—a vast honeycombed warehouse that's engineered to deliver hundreds of thousands of bursts of sweetness. Type in "Beck" and it leads you to Calexico. Type in "PJ Harvey" and you'll find Madder Rose. Mos Def introduces you to J-Live, Moby to Wolfsheim, the Feelies to the Boo Radleys. Why rail against Clear Channel when you can create the greatest college radio station in history right on your iMac? If you're prone to railing, of course, you can do so on your blog. There's a good chance that your blog uses services and software like TypePad and Movable Type, and you have Mena Trott to thank for that. She and her husband, Ben, run Six Apart, the entrepreneurial Bay Area tech company whose handiwork deserves much of the credit for bringing blogging to the masses. (Movable Type was originally called Serge, after the louche Gallic chansonnier Serge Gainsbourg. At thirty, Mena Trott may fall on the young side of the Gen-X spectrum, but this fact alone qualifies her as a true-blue member of the tribe.)

In 2001 an enterprising Brooklyn quirk specialist named Ze Frank recorded what he thought would be nothing more than an amusing birthday invitation. He called it "How to Dance Properly," and it consisted of Buster Keatonish black-and-white instructional footage of Frank showing off some jackass dance moves: the Who's Your Daddy?, the Make Love to the Crowd, the Stir the Pot of Love. Frank sent out a link to seventeen friends. They forwarded it to more. Within a few days millions of Web surfers around the world had watched "How to Dance Properly," and Frank decided to expand his site. Dropping by zefrank.com now is like gorging yourself at an all-you-can-eat snark buffet. There are public-service announcements, tongue-in-cheek news bulletins, interactive games and toys. The "Alien Performance Art" clip leads you to the five-second doodle scratch pad, which escorts you over to the "sing-along songs for children with short attention spans," and pretty soon you've squandered an afternoon. In the spring of 2006 he launched "The Show with Zefrank," a daily video blog whose social commentary could be so casually stinging that it made Stewart and Colbert look creaky.

If you're looking for an alternative to the *American Idol* monotony of mass culture at the start of the twenty-first century, this is where you'll find it. The new media of Generation X, in spite of its fundamental *newness*, gives us rich soil for incubating the home-grown and the handcrafted, the independent and the unfiltered—crucial and classically American qualities that have, over the past decade or so, been blotted out of the national conversation.

X

Few things embody that spirit of "a hundred million solutions" better than Meetup. Not long after the 9/11 terrorist attacks, a young tech entrepreneur named Scott Heiferman found himself flipping through *Bowling Alone*, Harvard scholar Robert D. Putnam's book about the disintegration of community in American life. "Although the big joke is that I never actually read the whole thing," Heiferman says. "I didn't have the attention span."

Heiferman grew up in Iowa. Thoughtful, bespectacled, and slightly built, he could be mistaken for a hip midwestern youth minister, and he is willing to go to great lengths to prevent himself from getting cut off from the regular folks of the American heartland. So serious is he about this, in fact, that soon after founding and running i-traffic, a nineties-boom Internet marketing company, he decided to experiment with what we might call "reslacking." He took a job in the service sector. *On purpose.* "I spend a lot of time with bankers, lawyers, Internet freaks, corporate wonks, and other people living strange lives," Heiferman later explained on his blog. "As a good marketing guy, that's a bad thing. And as a practicing anti-consumerist, that's a bad thing. I got a job at McDonald's to help get back in touch with the real world." When he says "Mc-Donald's," Heiferman does not mean that he accepted some "special projects guru" gig with Golden Arches corporate. No. He worked the counter at a real Mickey D's in New York City. He got paid $5.75 an hour. He burned his arms on the fry basket. "To actually work a tough fry-heaving, McNugget-wielding six-hour shift—and get home smelling like those fries and McNuggets—and realize that you only made about $30 that day . . . ," he later wrote. "That's a serious eye-opener."

Putnam's book—or, well, the first half of it—opened Heiferman's eyes even further, and it challenged him to come up with a remedy for American alienation. In 2002 Heiferman, with partners Matt Meeker, Peter Kamali, Brendan McGovern, Myles Weissleder, Greg Whalin, and millions of dollars in funding from eBay founder Pierre Omidyar, founded Meetup. It was based on a simple premise. If you had an interest in something (witchcraft, skateboarding, Chihuahuas, stinky cheese, knitting, Mission of Burma, Howard Dean), the Meetup site would help you find more people in your part of the country who had the same interest. All the Limburger-eating, feedback-friendly Wiccans in your town could gather at the Starbucks around the corner to bond. Meetup didn't set up the meeting. *You* did. You typed in your zip code, tracked down your fellow travelers, and decided where to meet. Meetup had no top-down authority over the proceedings. The site just served as a vehicle—a giant social networking hive that would let a thousand coffee klatches bloom.

Although Meetup attracted a lot of attention in the 2004 presidential campaign when Howard Dean's campaign team figured out how to use it to mobilize invisible armies of supporters, the site, in typical Gen-X fashion, has no core agenda of its own. In fact, when the founders finally got around to crafting a mission statement—four years after they'd launched the site itself—their reflexive Gen-X skepticism led to a few spats. An early draft of the statement contained the phrase "change the world." Brendan McGovern, the VP of finance and administration, couldn't stomach that. "He literally stood up in defiance," Heiferman remembers. "We were saying that the mission of the company was we want a meetup everywhere, about everything, to improve lives and change the world. And he just so defiantly *would not* accept the phrase. He said, 'It just rings so hollow, and it's a cliché,' but at least two of us said, 'No, that's the very reason why we should do it, because it flies in the face of the Gen-X thing.' It was literally *days* of fighting. We finally came around and got him to accept it, but it was kind of hilarious."

Heiferman's the first one to admit he's got "too much irony flowing through me." *Detachment, cynicism*—he doesn't happen to think those old Gen-X code words are off base. "It's not, 'Oh, the stereotype is wrong,' " he says. "I mean, the stereotype is *right*. But we've got to get past it." If you ask Heiferman whether Meetup *is* changing the world, he replies without hesitation, "Absolutely." It has to do with "small improvements in a lot of people's lives," he says. "Thinking really small, but with a lot of volume. You could say *that's* changing the world. And it's not *just* about improving lives in a small way, one by one. People having more power is changing the world. It gives anyone the power to organize around anything."

Still, early in 2007 Heiferman is feeling restless. As cool as it is to think of millions of vegan Vespa riders reaching out to each other through Meetup, the practice has so far failed to coalesce into something bigger. Out of it has arisen no lasting paradigm-shattering social movement. This concerns Heiferman. He wants to talk about it. He wants to talk about what a social movement *is* and how it might gather momentum in such a fractured, distracted, media-dominated society. He's feeling the same way he felt when he signed on as a McDonald's fry cook—he's eager to experiment. And so on a random Wednesday night in February he holds a meetup of his own, right there in the company's corporate office in New York City. He presides over it himself. Two dozen similarly restless men and women grab seats around a conference table, and Heiferman starts things off by telling them, "Thanks for participating in this random experiment. I have no idea where this is going to go."

Nobody does, but it's fascinating to hear the assembled congregants, most of them whip-smart Xers of the activist stripe, groping out loud to figure out what it would take for a large group of people to make something, *anything*, happen.

". . . There's something out of whack and so people just start talking and thinking about things . . ."

". . . voices that are not yet heard but are trying to be heard . . ."

". . . the society around you puts this intense pressure on you to conform . . ."

". . . There's always someone willing to make a major sacrifice . . ."

". . . we're going to destroy either each other or the environment . . ."

". . . texting is going to be huge, it's going to be a viral thing where you can actually mobilize people . . ."

"Because of technology," one young woman says, "we'll probably see more movements. People will just realize that they have the ability to make an impact. Look, how quickly did this meetup come together?"

"But what the hell are we doing?" Heiferman gently replies. "We're just talking."

A few days later Heiferman tells me that the Wednesday-night meetup helped him get a little closer to understanding something, something that's nagged at his conscience for a while now. It has to do with the idea of joining—the anxiety that it stirs up in people. At Meetup, whenever they talk about using the word *join* anywhere on the site (as in, "Hey, folks, are you interested in joining this group of Chihuahua lovers?"), debates rage throughout the office. To come out and join something—apparently that's such a loaded, polarizing concept that it might send thousands of Web surfers fleeing for Defamer. "It's such a scary word, to say 'join.'

It's just a terrifying word," Heiferman says. "By joining you're going to make your identity concrete, and that's scary. It's comfortable to stay on the sidelines, and more importantly, it's really fun to be able to make fun of everyone. I'm guilty of that. That is the comedic culture that we're in. If all of a sudden you've *joined* something, well, that means that you are one of the people to be made fun of."

And yet, if Xers were to set aside their skepticism and sarcasm long enough to band together behind an important issue, Heiferman says, the impact could be impressive. "The vision to me is very, very clear," he says. "There are going to be new organizations in the twenty-first century. They're going to emerge, they're going to be chapter-based, and I want it to happen. It's so obvious that people need to think about a movement, not just a bunch of actions.

"There's a bunch of things that the Internet has done," he goes on. "We can now publish anything, we can know anything, we can buy anything, we can sell anything. But we've not begun to see this notion of what collective action is. I think that's where it's going. Down the line you're going to see that 'you' become 'us' and 'we.' It is very much 'you' right now. But what gets interesting is when there's group power."

Life and How to Live It

> Every raw material at hand
> Remember all the things you said you'd do?
> What happens next?
> What happens now?
>
> —*Mission of Burma, "Learn How"*

I want to talk about James Brown.
I also want to talk about Henry James.

Theoretically, it should be difficult to talk about both of them at the same time, because no two human beings in the history of civilization have been more diametrically opposed—in taste, in temperament—than Henry James and James Brown. When you think of Henry James, the meticulous literary craftsman who gave us mandarin, word-dense novels such as *The Wings of the Dove* and *The Golden Bowl*, you think of a repressed Gilded Age fussbudget, a man of penetrating intellect who probably never got around to having sex with anyone. As a writer, James was prone to luminously clogged utterances such as this one: "He had thought himself, so long as nobody knew, the most disinterested person in the world, carrying his concentrated burden, his perpetual suspense, ever so quietly, holding his tongue about it, giving others no glimpse of it nor of its effect upon his life, asking of them no allowance and only making on his side all those that were asked."

James Brown, as a writer, was prone to utterances along the lines of "B*AYYYAYAYAYAYABEEEEE*eee*YAH!*" When you think of Brown you think of a reckless, pompadoured dervish, a sluice of primal energy who rushed past all that inward contemplation and let his genius geyser out in a prolonged shriek onstage at the Apollo Theater. You think of burnt-rubber car chases through the skunk-cabbage swamps of South Carolina. You think of that timeless mug shot where his hair has come unglued and the godfather of soul looks like a deranged Smurf on a Dexedrine bender. If Henry James sits enthroned as the ultimate American navel-gazer, James Brown preferred to focus his attention a few inches lower, which is not to slight his accomplishment in the least. Entire genres of American music—funk, go-go, hip-hop—would barely exist without him.

They both have things to teach us—the eunuch and the goat, the disembodied brain floating in a formaldehyde tank and the atomic-funk imp glazed with shiny sweat.

Let's start with "The Beast in the Jungle." James published "The Beast in the Jungle," a novella, over a century ago, in 1903, but it still has the power to scare the shit out of you. There's no beast in the story—at least nothing with fangs and claws and flammable breath—but it'll still creep you out worse than the torture scenes in *Saw III*. "The Beast in the Jungle" introduces us to a young man named John Marcher, one of those frail, neurasthenic protagonists who seemed to descend upon fin de siècle lawn parties like gnats. Roaming through a grand old house full of heirlooms and finery, Marcher comes upon May Bartram, a charming lass with whom he'd once had a vague flirtation in Italy. That was ten years before, and Marcher barely remembers it, but May Bartram stirs his memory of their meeting and reminds Marcher of something he told her back then, something dramatic and haunted and frankly kind of goth. A premonition! This is what John Marcher told May Bartram in Italy: that someday *something would happen to him*. Something huge. Something cataclysmic. Something beastly that would jump out of a manicured hedge and rip him to shreds. He'd begun to see it as "the thing."

As the two meet again, Marcher assures May Bartram that *the thing* hasn't happened yet. He's waiting. "Only, you know, it isn't anything I'm to *do*, to achieve in the world, to be distinguished or admired for," he tells her. "I'm not such an ass as *that*. It would be much better, no doubt, if I were."

"It's to be something you're merely to suffer?" Bartram asks him.

This is how he responds: "Well, say to wait for—to have to meet, to face, to see suddenly break out in my life; possibly destroying all further consciousness, possibly annihilating me; possibly, on the other hand, only altering everything, striking at the root of all my world and leaving me to the consequences, however they shape themselves."

And so, toward the end of this conversation, John and May make a pact. She will wait *with* him. She will, as a loyal friend, accompany John Marcher through the years as he anticipates the arrival of the beast. They wait and wait and wait. Leave it to Henry James to turn the mere act of sitting around waiting into a source of exquisite tension. Nothing, of course, happens. Murder, bankruptcy, addiction, a volcanic explosion, a slide into sexual depravity, a road-to-Damascus flash of spiritual enlightenment—nope, not one of these extravagant plot twists befalls John Marcher. Eventually, after many years have passed and May Bartram has died, he stands at her grave, and it's there that it dawns on him. "No passion had ever touched him, for this was what passion meant; he had survived and maundered and pined, but where had been *his* deep ravage?" James writes. "The extraordinary thing we speak of was the sudden rush of the result of this question. The sight that had just met his eyes named to him, as in letters of quick flame, something he had utterly, insanely missed, and what he had missed made these things a train of fire, made them mark themselves in an anguish of inward throbs. He had seen *outside* of his life, not learned it within . . . he had been the man of his time, *the* man, to whom nothing on earth was to have happened."

The Beast was inaction. The Beast was indecision. The Beast was hesitation. The Beast was *the very act of sitting around waiting for something to happen.* "The Beast had lurked indeed," Henry James tells us, "and the Beast, at its hour, had sprung."

Now let's get back to James Brown. After the godfather of soul died, at the age of seventy-three, on Christmas Day 2006, I found myself reading Gerri Hirshey's cover story about him in *Rolling Stone.* It was late at night, and I figured I was too zonked to read the whole thing, but I realized pretty quickly that I couldn't put it down. Hirshey knew James Brown for two decades. She spent substantial time with him. "Hanging with JB was a life-altering, if challenging, adventure," she wrote. "He would call when he hit Manhattan, stop his limo across from my apartment and pop out to hold up traffic until I was aboard." She wrote about James Brown weeping at Elvis Presley's coffin, dancing demonically to "Night Train" on *The TAMI Show*, writing the lyric "Say it loud! I'm black and I'm proud!" during some bloodshot frenzy after midnight in a Los Angeles hotel room—and then hauling off to a studio to record the song, *that night*, with thirty kids from Watts. She wrote about a life lived with cell-bursting, blood-sapping, heel-blistering, diabetes-baiting, eardrum-numbing, aorta-battering intensity. She wrote about live performances that took him to the very edge of obliteration. "JB re-enacted his own death-by-desire every time he took the stage and barked, 'Hit me!' to his dangerously sharp band," she wrote. "Each performance cost him seven to ten pounds, some of it sweat straight through the soles of his pointy-toed boots. And if he took the stage like a prince, he left it like a shipwreck survivor: Blood seeped from punished knees; the inflated, sculpted hair drooped like licorice. . . ."

Even in his seventies, James Brown never stopped dropping to his knees onstage. It's those knees I want to focus on. Because later in the story, Gerri Hirshey shared a private encounter with Mr. Dynamite—an encounter that's haunted me ever since I read about it. "One day," she wrote, "on the cusp of yet another 'comeback,' James pulled up his suit pants and insisted I inspect his knees, which looked worse than those of a retired linebacker, scarred, swollen and discolored."

Now ask yourself: What's the way to go out? Like John Marcher, dandified in spats and an ascot, staring at a hole full of dirt, bent over with regret over things undone? Or like James Brown—bruised, crunched, Quasimodally damaged, and yet proud of having kept nothing in storage, having emptied out the arsenal, having swallowed life like a mescal worm, having left a deep and long-lasting imprint upon the world?

Look, I'm no stranger to inertia. I have regrets. I'm *tired*. I'm writing this and I'm forty and my two kids are downstairs screaming at the top of their lungs, and there are moments when I'm fucking exhausted and paralyzed and the very idea of working *harder*, of delivering *more*, of *saving the world*, strikes me the way it probably strikes you when it's late and you finally just got the kids into bed and there are smeared dishes tottering in the sink. Ridiculous, right? Nuts. But the price of inaction is too high. We've waited long enough. We're staring down problems—environmental, cultural, spiritual—that could bury everything we love. We've got the raw materials to do something about that. We're equipped. We're wary enough to see through delusional "movements"; we're old enough to feel a connection to the past (and yet we're unsentimental enough not to get all gooey about it); we're young enough to be wired; we're snotty enough not to settle for crap; we're resourceful enough to turn crap into gold; we're quiet enough to endure our labors on the margins; we're experienced enough to know that change *begins* on the margins. Beyond that, *we're all we got*. Nobody else is going to do it. All we've got to be willing to do is to drop to our knees like the godfather of soul—over and over, until we no longer wince, until we no longer even notice the scars.

The Bush crowd will be gone soon, and then we can pounce. Quit your job, piss away your savings, go green, go red, go blue, plant zucchini in your front yard, stencil political slogans on the aluminum siding of your house in the suburbs, burn Paris Hilton in effigy in the public square, pool forces, launch the bottle rocket, spam the White House, release the hounds. The other day my wife and I were in the kitchen with our kids. We were playing the Replacements. No, this wasn't meant as some hipster indoctrination session—*Let It Be* just happened to be lying around when we were boiling water and needed a lively way to divert the kids. We put on the CD and there it was, the first song, "I Will Dare," with its pogo-stick bass line and Paul Westerberg's sozzled rasp. I grabbed my infant son, Toby, and picked him up and watched him wobble around in wordless euphoria as I growled along. At that moment it struck me that even though the song's got absolutely nothing to do with a sense of mission, even though the song is about some desperate Minneapolis geezer trying to get a date, *still*, that phrase "I will dare"—there it is, right? There we have the only lesson worth imparting to anyone, individually or generationally. There we have, in three clipped syllables, a cure for paralysis, a way to eliminate regret, maybe even a way to fix things. *A way to keep things from sucking*. Dare.

ACKNOWLEDGMENTS

Dan Peres might be one of the last of the instinctual, impulsive, and classically inspired editors in American magazines. It is Dan, the editor in chief of *Details*, who has sent me to Siberia to write about a Russian violinist, to Utah to cruise around a polygamist compound, to Kentucky to watch bariatric surgeons slicing into obese people, to Philadelphia to drink martinis with a Mafia lawyer, to Jerusalem to break bread with a religious zealot, to the Hollywood Hills to spend a delightful evening at the home of Marilyn Manson, to Arizona to meet a man with drug-resistant tuberculosis, and to the snake-and-tick-infested woods of Mississippi to reenact scenes from the Vietnam War with a group of men with machine guns.

One day in February 2006, when my newborn son was only a few days old and I was too weak and exhausted to put up a fight, Dan called me at home with perhaps the strangest assignment of all: He wanted me to weigh in on Generation X. What, he asked, had *happened* to us? What, if anything, had Generation X really accomplished? That afternoon Dan put me on a speakerphone, and he and I hashed out the idea with two equally insightful editors at the magazine, Jessica Lustig and Pete Wells. That night, and for a couple of sleep-deprived days afterward, I holed myself up in our attic and chipped away at an essay. The first draft struck me as bizarre and unfiltered, and I couldn't be sure it was what Dan had in mind, but a short while after I had turned it in, Pete Wells called me at home and said the magazine was running it more or less verbatim.

That essay became the demon seed for this book, and I'm grateful to the generous and crafty Mr. Peres for goading me into doing it even though I probably should've been downstairs changing diapers and forging a lifelong bond with my kid. Dan's role as my own private Lorenzo de' Medici did not end there. As the book began to take shape, he gave me the time to work on it—even when it turned out that, inevitably, oops, *haha,* I had to ask for *a little more time* than I'd originally expected—and he stepped in heroically and continuously to give me whatever I needed, including (at one point) a hotel room. It is no mere figure of speech to say that I am indebted to him. I might just owe him everything.

Further support came from the entire editorial team at *Details.* This book wouldn't have taken concrete form without encouragement, guidance, and free luxury grooming products from many of the magazine's staffers, past and present. Among them I have to thank Diana Benbasset, Chris Mitchell, Andrew Essex, Rockwell Harwood, Brian Farnham, Bill Van Parys, Greg Williams, Katherine Wheelock, Todd Pruzan, Alex Bhattacharji, Ian Daly (test driver of fast cars and unlicensed purveyor of herbal remedies), Bart Blasengame, Kevin Gray, Kayleen Schaefer, Ece Ozturk, Erica Cerulo, Genevieve Roth, Tim Hodler, Clay Thurmond, Yaran Noti, Allison Mooney, Ruthie Baron, and those two steadfast editors who've put up with my panic attacks for half a decade now, Ms. Lustig and Mr. Wells. In fact, Pete and Jessica, along with John McAlley and Andy Ward, unknowingly formed a quartet—an ad hoc board of trustees that helped me figure out how to keep writing when none of my old habits and tics seemed to suffice. Andy saved my brain with a single phone call, and John, in particular, must be singled out. For many weeks McAlley was the only other person who saw portions of the manuscript, and it's no exaggeration to say that his X-ray insights and Zen-master bluntness rescued me, on more than one occasion, from rambling my way right off a cliff.

In some ways this book began brewing in December 1993, when another generous and inspired editor, Jim Seymore, called me at my shoe-box apartment in Santa Barbara and asked me if I wanted to move to New York and write about movies and music for *Entertainment Weekly*. Thanks to Jim, my eight years at *EW* gave me the chance to explore phenomena such as the indie film movement, and my scary-smart editors there became some of my closest friends. I'm grateful not only to Jim (and to his gracious successor, Rick Tetzeli), but to Pete Bonventre, Richard Sanders, Maggie Murphy, Mark Harris, Mary Kaye Schilling, the aforementioned John McAlley, Doug Brod, David Hajdu, Jay Woodruff, Cindy Grisolia, Albert Kim, Thom Geier, Marc Bernardin, Cable Neuhaus, Jess Cagle, and Jeannie Park. Similarly, my adventure on the Poetry Bus would never have transpired without the backing of some patron saints at the Poetry Foundation in Chicago. Emily Warn and Emily White called with an odd proposition in the late summer of 2006—"Would you want to ride through the Pacific Northwest with a bunch of poets?" (I said no. Minutes later, at their prodding, I came to my senses.) I thank them and the foundation's Michael Marcinkowski and Anne Halsey for allowing me to contribute in a small way to one of the best Web sites in America. I also thank Joshua Beckman, Matthew Zapruder, Travis Nichols, Monica Fambrough, Erin Belieu, and the rest of the folks on the bus for welcoming me on board even though they had no idea who I was.

Countless other friends, colleagues, sources, and family members supplied me with contact numbers, health-maintenance tips, irresponsibly expensive bottles of wine, and discreet taps on the shoulder. The coolest man alive, David Walker from the Art Center College of Design in Pasadena, had the insight and the balls to tell me early on, before I made a really dumb mistake, that I was completely wrong about something. David Browne patiently and painstakingly answered my every inquiry into the topic of "Um, What Is a Book?" Jeremy Toback told me why I needed to do this. Cameron Sinclair, in one stray sentence over breakfast, clarified what I needed to say. Jim Egen kept me from going nuts. Dennis Beasley kept me from going bankrupt. *Newsweek*'s Sid Hajari has continued to be nice to me over the years even though I embarrassed both of us by throwing up on the field during the Nine Inch Nails show at Woodstock II. Gobs of extra gratitude go to Rich Siefert, Alex Seldin, Jeff Samberg, Danny Castor, Steve Diamond, Justin Fox, Russ Spencer, Lisa Harper, Jenny Rosenstrach, Jon Wertheim, A. J. Jacobs, Danielle Claro, DeLauné Michel, Chris Nashawaty, Tom Junod, Keith Blanchard, Cary Darling, Gary Robb, Judy Bolch, Laura Galloway, David Kamp, Owen Gleiberman, Dave Daley, Sue Bunnell, H. T. Owens, Rick Reiken, Bronwen Hruska, Lawrence Severt, Sandy Gray, Holly Millea, Jess Walter, Whitney Terrell, Paul Stiles, Elizabeth Koch, Phil Whitney and Robin Helman, Matt Weingarden, Chris Raymond, Chuck Fontana, Rob Boynton, H. Robertson Barrett IV, Richard and Susan Gordinier, Curtis and Steffi Gordinier, Amy and David Regan, and the heavyweight champion of the world, John McPhee.

My unflappable god of research, Sean O'Heir, fielded my every request without complaint, even when said requests were fired off at two in the morning and might perhaps be phrased along the lines of "Hey, Sean, can you get me some clips about the Internet? By, like, Monday morning?"

My benefactors at Viking, Molly Stern and David Cashion, believed in this book from the start. What's even better is that they believed in it in the middle, too, and even at the end. Their enthusiasm did not flag. If everyone were blessed with editors like these, writers wouldn't have to drink so much. David Cashion is such a gentleman, such a model of good taste and humor and restraint, that I came to welcome his calls even when, *oh, you know*, just kind of wondering when I might finish the thing. His insights were illuminating. His suggestions were spot-on. He got me to lop off four-thousand-word sections of the first draft and somehow I never screamed in pain. *That's* genius.

My agent, Scott Waxman, has stood by me for ten years, and although we've been through a few setbacks and false starts together, he's never failed to back me up. He's an honorable dude and I am grateful for his wisdom, advocacy, and protection from the forces of evil. His teammates at the Waxman Agency, Farley Chase and Byrd Leavell, are always quick to answer questions and offer direction, while Melissa Sarver brings great elegance and speed to the task of handling my frazzled phone calls and sending me anything important and official.

All of these people helped, but only one person helped *all the time*, and that is my wife, Julie Schrader. It takes great patience to live with a writer. It takes much more than patience to live with a writer who is trying to complete a book. It takes something superhuman to do so when there are two young children in the house and the writer's involvement in their entertainment, hygiene, transportation, schooling, and feeding is limited at best. (I am certain that Julie often thinks there are *three* children in her care. She is not wrong about this.) She has heard me utter the tiresome phrase "Don't worry, I'm almost done" thousands of times over the past fourteen years, and even though she knows it is meaningless, and even though I often trudge around the house without having shaved or showered for several days, she has always, always been at my side with love and encouragement and striking beauty. She made brilliant and invaluable contributions to everything from the title to the cover of this book, and rarely did she ask for anything in return other than a few hours of *Gilmore Girls* and *Project Runway*. Saving the world is not some remote and ethereal concept to Julie. It is what she does, in her own crucial way, on a daily basis.

The Power of Riffage in the Ongoing Battle Against Melancholia and Torpor: A Brief Benediction

Now that we're done, I want to take a moment to thank two men who had nothing to do with this book.

Those men are Tom Scholz and Brad Delp. Cognoscenti, including the fellow members of my cabin at Camp Pinehurst in the summer of 1976, will recognize these names from the outset. Mr. Scholz, for those who don't know, was the visionary composer, producer, arranger, lyricist, and Mozartian multi-instrumentalist in Boston, the seventies band whose miniature symphonies of basement-baroque, arena-rock riffage were often dismissed, by pinched boomer critics of the era, as "faceless corporate rock." The late Mr. Delp was the singer. (Although that term, *singer*, seems far too small to describe the gale force of Mr. Delp's vocal instrument. *Lark*, perhaps. *Hurricane thrush. Cannonball cantor. Meistersinger!*)

Look, we get down. We get depressed. We are lucky, many of us, to have access to perks and privileges that previous societies in the course of human civilization would have bestowed only upon royals and Rothschilds. We have shelter and clean water. We have 401(k)s and 529s. We have cellular phones and computers. We have spicy tuna rolls. And still we get down.

Who is not susceptible to the melancholic humors of our age? Who has not felt him- or herself groping, during a day of domestic drudgery, for foreign words whose meaning we do not fully understand? Words like *anomie* and *tristesse, angst* and *weltschmerz, Sturm und Drang* and *saudade.* I am no different, my friends. I am not immune. In the course of attempting to write this manuscript I, too, suffered through many an overcast afternoon of angst-ridden anomie, and were it not for the restorative powers of (to use a random example) *Project Runway* (thank you, Tim Gunn, thank you so very much), this book might be coming to you posthumously, cobbled together out of my notes by a team of patient and telepathic editors.

But if there is a single cattle prod of inspiration that goaded me onward as I attempted to transfer the storms of my heart to paper, if there is a beckoning spirit who sought to rouse me in those moments when the struggles of my generation had forced me into the fetal position under my desk, that cattle prod of the beckoning spirit, or whatever, could be found in a song. And that song was and is and will be "Don't Look Back." By Boston.

> *Don't look back*
> *A new day is breakin'*
> *It's been too long since I felt this way*

O what sustenance I have found in those simple words. Yes, of course, the boomer critics and their snickering allies in American media tend to dismiss such lyrics as gormless self-help-shelf positivity, as *cheese,* but I can speak only to the truth of my own experience. I recall a day in late January when these lyrics, written by Tom Scholz and delivered with Wagnerian brio by Bradley Delp, lifted me out of my chair and compelled me to raise my fists to the sky in exultation. (That I accidentally slammed one of those fists into a lamp from Pier 1 is a mere footnote; I was too rapt to notice.) All of a sudden I did not yearn to scratch the psoriasis on my scalp. I did not, in that moment, pay any mind to the Styrofoam *squeak* of a sinus infection in my left ear, nor to the ulcer I was convinced I had nurtured right under my rib cage, nor to the hysterical caterwauling of my two children downstairs. I was levitated! I was transported! I was born anew! The malaise that had gripped me for days began to blow away like San Gabriel Valley smog on that rare day when you can actually see the mountains and your eyes don't feel as though they've been sprinkled with shards of glass. (Although people tell me that the smog in Southern California is not as bad as it used to be. When I was a kid riding my motocross bike to junior high, it felt like I was sucking hard on a pilot light. So my gratitude to you, too, Governor Schwarzenegger, and to your visionary predecessors in Sacramento.)

"Don't Look Back"! Indeed. If these lyrics are cheese, then, my friends, it is the fragrant curds of destiny we must once again embrace. Let it be cheese that rouses us from our stupor. Let *fromage* serve as our cri de coeur as we march forth to restore hope and equilibrium to a world gone mad. Smell the cheese. Breathe deep of the cheese. Go now, my friends, go to your computers and seek out the ninety-nine-cent transfusion of cheesed-out, neo-Nietzschean will to power that is Boston's "Don't Look Back." Here, perhaps, shall you and I locate our burning bush, our Plymouth Rock. With this wind of cheese at our backs we shall set goals, map out ten-year plans, launch movements, stand up for what's right, and disseminate tracts that bring the people of our benighted demographic niche unparalleled inspiration. Now is the time.

Play it as many times as feels necessary, comrades. Twice usually works for me.

To Tom and Brad—*Grazie. Dankeschön. Dōmo arigatō.*

Jeff Gordinier
Laguna Beach, Las Vegas, Westchester County

INDEX